Virtuous Woman

&

Virtuous Woman

*Reflections on
Christian Feminist Ethics*

Denise Lardner Carmody

ORBIS BOOKS

Maryknoll, New York 10545

The Catholic Foreign Mission Society of America (Maryknoll) recruits and trains people for overseas missionary service. Through Orbis Books, Maryknoll aims to foster the international dialogue that is essential to mission. The books published, however, reflect the opinions of their authors and are not meant to represent the official position of the society.

Library of Congress Cataloging-in-Publication Data

Carmody, Denise Lardner, 1935-
    Virtuous woman : theological reflections on Christian feminist
ethics / Denise Lardner Carmody.
        p.   cm.
    Includes bibliographical references and index.
    ISBN 0-88344-817-3
    1. Christian ethics—Catholic authors.   2. Feminist theology.
I. Title.
BJ1249.C1688   1993
241'.082—dc20   92-17952
                                                                      CIP

For Betty Creech

Contents

Preface

This book is basically a reflective theological essay on the current state of Christian feminist ethics. In the course of interacting with many current writers and recent works, I try to clarify (in the first instance, for myself) what the capitalized words in my subtitle imply. In other words, I try to work out what an ideal "Christian feminist ethics" would stress, value, try to achieve.

It turns out that I want Christian feminist ethics to be more Christian than what I tend to find. The feminist and ethical aspects of the programs I have contemplated are in relatively good shape. Regularly, however, the Christian aspect bears pondering, criticism, even lamentation. Others will have to judge to which political category this conclusion belongs. My intent is to be neither liberal nor conservative. I dislike such labels, as do many writers, and I despise ideology, which seems to me a closure of soul.

Still, readers should be forewarned on several headings, lest they misunderstand the character of this book. It is not a survey of contemporary Christian feminist ethics. It is not an essay developing principal positions for a systematic Christian feminist ethics. It is a series of soundings, a paging through interesting books and articles, that makes no attempt to represent the whole of any author's work, but rather meditates on striking texts. I do not believe any of these texts is ripped out of context, but I am not interested in giving seminars on the entirety of any author's corpus.

Readers should also be forewarned that in making theological critiques I bring to bear as my main instrument a high Christology—that is, the traditional Christian conviction that Jesus is fully divine, as well as fully human. I believe that this

Christology is necessary for orthodox Christian faith, and that embracing it relegates many current approaches to Christian feminism to the realm of the highly dubious. For example, I cannot accept without heavy qualification the much bruited feminist criterion of "women's experience," whether of Jesus or other things. To make women's experience the decisive say in one's worldview seems to me unchristian. We, women or men, are but creatures of a day. Most of our current slogans will end up in the dustbin of history. What endures in Christianity is the stunning sacramentality of Jesus, expressed in the gospels and proposed as faith in the creeds. One has only to read the Gospel of John straightforwardly to see that this sacramentality comes from Jesus' being the divine Word become flesh. One has only to read the patristic literature and the medieval mystics held dear by the Church catholic to see that the divinity of Christ is the great linchpin of tradition. For example, Julian of Norwich makes no sense without this conviction.

Like the crucifixion and resurrection of Jesus, the divinity of Jesus is "a stumbling block to the Jews and to the Gentiles foolishness." Ironically, though, it is the center that has held through the Christian centuries, while various vogues and fads have come and gone. So it is the center of my critiques, sometimes tacit, sometimes expressed, as I move eclectically, perhaps abruptly, through such topics of current Christian feminist ethical interest as commitment, discernment, social ethics, sexual morality, and ecclesiastical issues.

Finally, readers should be warned that although most of the sections in this book deal with matters intramural to Christian feminist ethicists I have on occasion deliberately used materials bearing on such topics as secular feminism, Jewish feminism, or the plight of women in India. The reason is to break out of the Christian ghetto and remind all of us that both virtue and vice are alive and well outside the Christian gates.

My main debt is to the many Christian feminist writers doing admirable work today. I would also like to thank the staff at Orbis Books; my secretary, Betty Creech; my students in courses on Women and World Religions; and my husband, John Carmody, who, as always, has been my first reader and editor.

～§ 1 §～

Introduction

[In a fine novel by Ellen Gilchrist, Anna, a talented writer, leaves a cancer ward where her best friend has just died, hand in her hand, and phones her lover.] Two hours later she was in Phillip's arms in a room in the Plaza Hotel. "Everything seems so fragile," she said. "In the face of that I guess we at least get to spend a night together every now and then. You can stay all night, can't you?"

"I can stay all night. I'm in trouble over you, Anna. I think it's going to get worse. Because after this nothing will happen." He held her very close to him, her body was enclosed in his. He counted the seconds of his sadness and his happiness. He was enlarged and diminished and broken and made whole. It made no sense to him but he came when she called him. It did not happen often now.

"I love you to the breadth, depth, height. I love you whether I see you or not. If I don't see you, I still love you. Remember that." She leaned over him and kissed his forehead, his eyelids and earlobes and the hollow places of his neck. Then she got out of bed and turned on all the lights and came back to him and made love to him like a cheerleader of love, like a panther of love, in view of being alive, of breathing without pain, in the

1

light of being cognizant and alive she took the married man along and they made love.[1]

Is Anna a good woman, a woman of virtue? That is where I would like to begin. Let us assemble the evidence. She has stayed with her dying friend to the last, offering her what solace she could. She has not fled from pain and death. Though she does not know what she believes about death, afterlife, God, she has stayed this part of the course. Without her, her friend's death probably would have been more painful. Still, Anna has paid a price for her generosity. Her own life, all life, seems more embattled, more threatened, and so more precious. What can she do to shore up her spirits? How can she fight off despair?

Instinctively she calls her lover, whom she now sees rarely. He is a doctor, a pediatrician. Whenever she calls, he comes to her, because she is like nothing else in his life. Now he comforts her against the fragility of life. Other times he simply delights in her beauty, her vitality. The trouble he is in over her is love. When she goes definitively, nothing else of significance will happen to him. With her, he becomes both more and less, both broken and whole. His love is beyond reason, makes no sense.

She loves him totally, as though he were burned into her soul. Now her way of gaining comfort, of beating back her dark thoughts, is to comfort him. Tenderly she kisses all the pieces of him. Then a great desire to assert their being alive together comes over her and she treats him to a performance of sexual love. With unusual clarity, heightened awareness of every implication, she renews their adulterous passion.

Anna is typically secular. She goes to no Church, obeys no religious code. She has had several marriages and numerous lovers. She is always butting into the business of other members of her large, disorganized family clan. She is a gifted, disciplined, successful writer. She left convent school at fourteen because the restrictions chafed, left no place for her creativity. She wants to live fully, in face of an instinctive awareness that she is dying. Beyond the dying that is ordinary aging, she is in the first phases of her own cancer, as she knows, though not clearly. Eventually she will commit suicide. Her strength will run out. Confronted with advanced cancer, she will decide to end her life as a free act. Yet while she lives she lights the world aglow. When she dies those who loved her will feel part of themselves has gone.

I cannot answer the question of Anna's virtue simply. Even if I knew more about her, I'd have to say that the goodness and evil, the grace and sin in her life, tally to sums known only to God. But I like Anna. I forgive her most of her failings because she wants to celebrate life. Her work, her affairs, her dealings with her family seem like nothing so much as efforts to say yes to creation, and so to say yes to creation's source. She lives in the midst of tangles from which she can never free herself. All the relations in her family are slanted. Each has been thrown out of true by years of compromise, imperfection, mutual accommodation. The same is true of her affair with the pediatrician. He is and is not good to his wife. Anna does and does not regret complicating, perhaps ruining, his marriage. Nothing in the morality of Anna's life is simple, obvious. She is a wonderful character, because her voice sings so clearly our common refrain. We do not know the most important things. We cannot be simple in any way, let alone simply good.

But is this common refrain necessarily true? Are there not ways that we can become simple, perhaps even simply good? Not for Anna, who knows nothing about divinization. Not for any people shaped through and through by secular cultures. But perhaps, with many qualifications, for people shaped through and through by Christian faith. Perhaps for people working consistently to take to heart, to conscience, the gift of divine life proclaimed in the gospels. So the first thing we should think about, as we embark on this essay in Christian feminist ethics, is the *perhaps* that the gospels introduce. Standing at the border of reason and faith, it may be enough for us to begin by saying that embracing Christ might make all the difference—might radically change the consciousness of people like Anna.

How might such a change appear? It might have both external and internal aspects. Would it take Anna away from the hospital bed of her dying friend? Surely not. Her being there is a great sign of her goodness of heart and courage. Would it alter her sense of what her friend's dying entails? Surely it would. It would both deepen the pathos of her friend's suffering by assimilating her to the crucified Christ, and transpose the entire situation by relocating it in the patterns of Christ's resurrection. Indeed, it might even make these alterations gracefully, agreeing to the fierce demands of Anna's artistic integrity, her deep passion to love those closest to her whether she sees them or not.

Might Christian faith alter Anna's relation with her lover, the married pediatrician? It might indeed. Her zest and tenderness might strengthen, because she could be more aware of the divine Spirit loving in her love. Her troubles about the adultery would have to sharpen, perhaps to the point where she would judge the relationship insupportable, though still the most consoling thing in her repertoire. Unless Anna were to become deeply intimate with God, Christian faith would probably not reconcile her to calling her liaison completely wrongheaded. Until she found a purer love, she could feel entitled, even obliged to hold onto this one, thinking God has to be the goodness in all loves, even those that should not and for mature faith finally cannot be.

Finally, how might a Christian Anna come to think about her own hastening death? What might the messages from her wayward blood cells tell her about her meaning, and being? She just might sense that accepting these messages as the dispositions of her God could be her purification. Following the messages, the intimations of her approaching death, that encouraged her to hate the destruction of life, even counseled her to rage against it, she could find a passage to self-abandonment. Naked she had come from her mother's womb. Naked she would return. Whether she returned sooner or later she could leave in God's hands as a gift, a return of grace. And if she connected these dispositions, cribbed from Job, to the dispositions of the Christ she, as a mature Christian, had come to love above all else, she might be glad to suffer and die. Suffering and dying might beckon as a way to be closer to him, more intimate.

All that would be asking a lot of Anna and Christian faith. Simple observation tells us that only saints attain a healthy desire to suffer. Yet the New Testament tells us that all Christians are saints. Whether deeply or only shallowly, all live beyond themselves, from depths that are not their own. Their identities, their meanings, depend on God more than themselves. Their lives are hidden with Christ in God. So, generous Christians will say, are hidden the lives of all God's people, whether explicitly Christian or not. To be human is to rest in the hands of God, day and night to receive calls from God to say yes to offers of love. Christians have the wonderful, irreplaceable witness of Christ on which to anchor this conviction, but God has not left the offer of divine love, which is divine life, without witness anywhere. Anna's secularism is no defeat of God. Her self-indulgence, ignorance, even despair of life with a mortal illness are not the last word. Though she may be a sinner, that does not determine her standing with God. God loves us; God's Son was given for us. When we lack virtue, God makes the divine virtue supply for our deficiency.

O lovely Anna. If only you had known the things for your peace. And yet, lovely Anna, passionate Anna, Anna brimming with life, perhaps in your own way, in God's unique way for you, you did know these things. Perhaps your gamble on love pleased God exceptionally. Perhaps all that you tried to do for your family, in your work, from your love of life, expressed the imprint of God better than the gray words and works of people with better reputations. There's a mystery about your goodness, your virtue, your life. There's a challenge to all thoughtful people. Christian faith, the ethical life, genuine feminism—each has much to learn from you, as well as much to teach us about what you might mean.

Unless we begin our reflections on Christian feminist ethics with a willingness to learn from the experiences of others—like Anna—without putting on the blinders of facile and presumptuous judgments, our reflections are not likely to take us very far. No mortal can gain insight by pontificating about God's judgments; any person of significant faith has to try to look upon other people with God's eyes, which Christ tells us are wholly loving. Indeed, the beginning of Christian ethics is wonder at the generosity of the Lord. If Anna was a prodigal who returned, God was sure to be thrilled, to order the servants to kill the fatted calf, put rings on her fingers, call in her friends, make merry. If we, evil as we are, know how to give our children good things, how much more would God have wanted to give good things to Anna, God's child! Anna had only to say yes, please, if you will.

Perhaps she did. Perhaps her suicide was a profound petition that God take her away from this wretched world of cancers and half-loves, spotty beginnings and imperfect endings. Perhaps it was a fierce hope that God would wipe away every tear from her eye and death would be no more. Any adequately Christian assessment of Anna's actions has to reckon with this possibility. Any fully Christian assessment has to place it front and center. How could the news of Christ be good for Anna? What could the abiding of Father, Son, and Spirit in her depths have worked, to crown her life with the most beautiful of gifts? That is how saints have to pursue ethical inquiries. That is what the blood of Christ shed for Anna requires.

Feminist Ethics

Marilyn Pearsall defines ethics and, more specifically, feminist ethics, as follows:

Ethics is the philosophy of morality and, with esthetics, makes up the centrality of the area of philosophy called axiology (value theory). Ethics is concerned with questions of right and wrong conduct, the nature of moral obligation, and the notion of the good life. The core question, posed by Aristotle, is "What kind of life shall I best lead?"

Feminist ethics starts, in one sense, with the realization that Aristotle's famous question in "male-stream" philosophy does not—or has not—applied to women. As de Beauvoir says, women have been objects and not subjects. By that she means that women have been denied

the right to be full moral agents; they have not been those who "choose a life."

Feminist ethics, therefore, now poses the question: Is it good for women? (This is a recurring question in the feminist manifestoes of the second wave.) In this way, feminist theorists are seeking the re-visioning of moral philosophy. The feminist imperative is to challenge the hegemony of male ethical theory and to insist on "the woman's voice."

Feminist ethics, then, arises directly out of women's lives and women's issues. (These had been given only passing consideration in patriarchal value theory.) For example, we see much concern with reproductive rights, since these reflect the centrality of women's demand for control over "our bodies, ourselves." The moral issues concerning abortion have been, accordingly, the subject of significant analysis by feminist philosophers. Paradigmatic of female sexual autonomy, abortion issues affect all women, directly or indirectly.[2]

Feminist ethics, like all ethics, is concerned with right and wrong. To meet this concern, it has to contend with moral obligation: What weighs on the healthy conscience? What do mature, good people feel is binding? Broadened, this concern, this contention, raises the question of the good life. For Aristotle, the good life is not the life of sensual pleasure. It has nothing to do with a fat bank account, lazy afternoons by the pool at the club. It is the life that is worthy of the human spirit. It is the life that honors the unique status of human beings as rational animals, living things that create meaning through inner and outer words.

Aristotle made metaphysics the ballast of his ethical inquiries. In the footsteps of Plato, he thought that contemplation was the highest human activity, and that the end (*telos*) contemplation was to become as much like God as possible Feminist ethics, according to the authority we have quoted, has no truck with this ballast. Whether becoming much like God as possible is merely an idiosyncrasy of "

stream" philosophy or applies equally to women is not a matter of interest.

However true it may be that throughout the history of ethical theorizing women have been objects rather than subjects, what should we say now about the end of women's ethical inquiries? Ought women, too, to be contemplative? Is the proper conclusion of women's studies of the kind of life they ought to lead the realization that God is the unmoved mover of their every striving, or should we consign this Aristotelian notion to the dustbin of a patriarchal past? If so, then what new, different finality ought to direct women's choosing of their lives? What new highest good ought to illumine their moral activity, help them live in the light rather than darkness, in the truth rather than foolishness?

To pose the question, Is it good for women?, we have to know what women are, where their fulfillment lies. Few of the feminist manifestoes of any wave help us gain this knowledge. Most prescind completely from questions of wherefrom and whereto, of women's beginning and women's end. In this the manifestoes are merely modern, or postmodern, and secular. In this they merely ape the reigning mentality in academic philosophy, which is agnostic about creation and destiny, if not uninterested.

Still, the questions remain. It is not enough to mandate bracketing matters of creation and destiny. The mandating ought to be rational, defended—and the natural drive that Aristotle placed at the core of being human ("all people by nature desire to understand") says that it cannot be defended. Any arbitrary limiting of the human spirit's questioning is a betrayal of what we human beings are most intimately. Any veto of our interest in where we came from and where we are going is sacrilegious—an effort to twist our best reality out of joint.

It is wonderful to insist on the imperative to challenge the hegemony of any philosophy exclusively male, neglectful of women, or disdainful toward women. All just people have the obligation to listen to women's voices and honor fully the dual sexuality of humankind. But I cannot call this imperative radically feminist unless it deals with the deepest roots of wom-

en's humanity. When feminist philosophers pretend that the roots of women's humanity are unmysterious and require no selfless contemplation of depths beyond what pragmatic, instrumental reason can sound, I find them inadequate, even superficial.

The most significant datum about women, as about men, is that we do not furnish our own reason to be. Taken on our own, apart from the mystery that classical philosophy considered divine, we are opaque, ultimately uninteresting ephemera. How radical or passionate can a philosophy of moral action and being that ignores this elementary reality be?

It is dubious, then, whether current feminist ethics arises directly out of the depths of women's lives and concerns. It is open to debate whether the description that introduces this section (and the readings that it introduces accurately) can pass muster before philosophers or general readers who are not agnostic, atheistic, or ideologically closed to classical Greek philosophy, biblical wisdom, and Asian philosophy.

Certainly patriarchal cultures, dominated by the interests of men, have neglected the sex-specific interests of women. Certainly history comes down to us warped, inasmuch as women's voices have not told the substories as frequently as men's. But we do ourselves no favors by assuming that women's lives and issues are not as centered by the divine mystery at the heart of patriarchal value theory as men's. We miss the heart of the human matter when we take as our defining antagonist a male chauvinism limited to cultural hegemony.

And finally, we do ourselves no favor when we make reproductive rights the first word of feminist ethics. If women are not their wombs; if women (contrary to Aristotle) have fully human souls; then the first rights that should concern us are those stemming from women's deepest capacities, hungers, needs to know and love—from women's souls. The control that women rightly seek over their bodies and their selves is exactly parallel to that which men rightly seek. It cannot be a complete autonomy, because no human being exists in isolation. It cannot be a heteronomy, because every human soul or spirit stands free of crowd control. It has to be a theonomy, a moral law compatible with and informed by the divine mystery holding and defining each human being.

Now, having voiced some objections, let us treat feminist ethics as we treated Anna, with our best intimations of the love and goodness of the Christian God. We recall, first, that orthodox Christian faith never despises the material world or the cultural worlds that human beings fashion. Because the Word of God took flesh, the first word of believers ought to be positive, welcoming. We should sympathize with any well-meaning feminist ethics, even when we have to criticize its foundations. Were secular feminist ethicists to reflect more adequately on the personal origins of women's discontents and the kinds of fulfillment that these discontents imply, much of what they suggest for the reworking of values and culture would become more useful.

Second, we ought to admit from the outset that Christianity deserves much of the blame for the irreligious character of most present-day feminist ethics. In many historical periods, including the recent centuries, the Churches have not championed women's cultural rights. They have not sought women's freedom, development of their potential, or equal opportunity with men to gain satisfaction, fulfillment, and happiness. The tendency of male Church leaders has been to tell women what to do, how to live, and what their proper roles are, rather than to listen to women or help women discern the lessons of their own experience. Even as we say that Christianity has championed the dignity of women as full children of God, we must complain that the sexism of Church leaders has caused much suffering and tolerated more.

Third, because God has left witnesses to the divine wisdom and love everywhere, feminist ethicists deserve a patient hearing. Whatever their defects, we overlook their intentions at our peril. God has made all human beings for freedom. For freedom Christ has set us free (Gal 5:1). Inasmuch as the great passion of contemporary feminist ethics is freedom, Christians ought to understand most of its longings, frustrations, and programs. Understanding much, Christians ought to forgive much and to forge alliances at all points possible.

Christian Feminist Ethics

Christian ethics is the effort to direct the actions of the followers of Christ so that they are consistent with faith in him, commitment to his gospel, and the flourishing of the divine life that he communicates. As well, it is the effort to clarify questions of right and wrong, of healthy and unhealthy values, by Christian faith. In my understanding of the term, Christian ethics is a branch of Christian theology; it is faith seeking understanding, in this case, understanding of moral matters. Thus, I will use the terms *Christian ethics* and (Christian) *moral theology* interchangeably.

The entry on feminist ethics in *The Westminster Dictionary of Christian Ethics* can open our discussion of Christian feminist ethics:

> In its most general sense "feminist ethics" refers to any ethical theory that locates its roots in feminism, and especially in the contemporary feminist movement. Feminism, in its most fundamental meaning, is a conviction and a movement opposed to discrimination on the basis of gender. It opposes, therefore, any ideology, belief, attitude, or behavior that establishes or reinforces such discrimination. In terms of social structure, feminism is opposed primarily to patriarchy. The ultimate aim of feminism is equality among persons regardless of gender. Since discrimination on the basis of gender (sexism) is perceived by feminists as pervasively discrimination against women, feminism aims to correct this bias by a bias for women. This includes a focal concern for the well-being of women and a taking account of women's experience as a way to understand what well-being means for women and men.[3]

I find this description of feminism both clear and, in the main, unobjectionable. It represents accurately how I understand feminism and why I call myself a feminist. I think that all ethicists ought to be feminists of this stripe, because I think all ethicists have a personal as well as a professional obligation to justice. Justice is in good measure opposition to discrimination, promotion of what is fair. To discriminate against women, or men, on the basis of their gender (the cultural impact of their sex) is to be unfair—to deny the equal humanity of the sexes.

I believe that no reference to Scripture, tradition, or secular customs can rightly deny the equal humanity of women and men. To my mind such a denial flies in the face of biology, common sense, and the creative activity of God. Rightly, then, do feminists oppose ideologies, beliefs, attitudes, and behaviors that establish or reinforce sexual discrimination. Reason and faith conspire to support such opposition, and so to mandate feminism. As long as feminism means a movement to promote equality among human beings regardless of their gender, it seems to me a necessary corollary of a proper understanding of how God made women and men, how Christ treated women and men, and how the followers of Christ ought to treat women and men.

Inasmuch as *patriarchy* means a rule of men over women that promotes inequality or frustrates equality, it is not only the natural enemy of feminism but also the enemy of what I take to be the gospel of Christ. If a culture calling itself Christian is patriarchal in this pejorative sense, it is inauthentic. If a Church is patriarchal, so organized or administered that it discriminates on the basis of gender, it is inauthentic. Sexism is a sin. It distorts reality and hurts human beings, who are made in the image and likeness of God. Because it is composed of fallible human beings, the Christian Church can be sinful and has been so frequently.

It is no surprise, then, to find that the Christian Church has been sexist in the past and continues to be so today. Sexism is one face of our significant sinfulness, one of the many ways in which we Christians fail our sinless master. To want a Church free of patriarchy is a holy desire, a source of proper reform. Far from finding feminism incompatible with loyal membership in Christ's Church, I find it a necessary expression of loyal membership. How can people commit themselves to Christ, the sun of justice, and refrain from opposing injustice based on gender? How can they put asunder what God has joined: faith and justice? Only, I would say, through underdevelopment or hypocrisy.

The only qualification I would enter to the description of feminism that I have been glossing occurs at the sentence, "Since discrimination on the basis of gender (sexism) is perceived by feminists as pervasively discrimination against women, feminism aims to correct this bias by a bias for women." The qualification is minor. It seems to me clear that women have suffered more from sexism than men. In fact, the majority of cultures throughout history have been patriarchal—controlled by men to the disadvantage of women. Feminists, whether female or male, are only being realistic when they make this perception of bias the basis for their ethical analyses and programs.

However, it is a delicate operation to correct a bias by taking an opposite bias. If we stick to a simple, geometric image, the matter seems easy: the ship has been tilting at a forty-five degree angle; to get it upright we need only tilt it forty-five degrees in the opposite direction. But cultural activity is more complicated. The people doing both the computations of biases and the work of trying to correct them are not perfect. Nor can the attitudes of human beings be shifted right or left with ease. As with affirmative action to correct distortions introduced by racism, taking a bias in favor of women requires constant surveillance if it is not to become a counter-bias in the pejorative sense.

Such a pejorative counter-bias is more than an inclination to favor or focus primarily upon women. It is also an inclination to think ill of men, work against perceived male interests, and ultimately deny that men are the equals of women in possessing humanity, being images of God. At that point one has to speak of reverse sexism, just as when affirmative action meant to help blacks becomes prejudice against whites, one has to speak of reverse racism. These are subtle dangers and evils compared to the gross biases that blacks and women have suffered, but they require our attention. Indeed, in circles of what is sometimes called radical feminism, the plain fact seems to be that men are often objects of derision if not contempt and hatred. No feminism compatible with Christian faith can make its bias for women into a destructive bias against men.

Last, I find the focal concern of an acceptable feminism for the well-being of women both logical and admirable. Similarly, I find the effort to use women's experience to understand what well-being means for both sexes something entailed in any mature, generous commitment to promoting the cultural equality of women and men. Implicit here is a bisexual understanding of human nature. Contrary to the errors of both patriarchy and radical feminism, women and men are oriented to one another ineluctably. Naturally, this orientation is not ironclad, determining all people at all times. On the whole, though, I find acknowledging it plain biological wisdom and cultural health. In terms of Christian faith, I find it the corollary of the account of creation given in Genesis and fully compatible with Paul's insight (Gal 3:28) that in Christ there is neither male nor female (superiority).

The efforts of feminists to learn from the experiences of women what human nature needs for its full flourishing are bound to impinge upon men. The sexes cannot become healthier in isolation. It may be useful for a given man or woman to move away from the other sex for a shorter or longer time, as it may be useful for any individual to move away from society at large for a patch of solitude. But overall, in terms of the patterns we have to consider customary, even normative, men and women need one another and do well to want to be in one another's company. Indeed, the desire for healthy heterosexual relations is one of the most poignant cries of the human heart, echoing in every generation as a plea to God for salvation.

When it comes to specifically Christian feminist ethics, our source says the following:

> Some feminist ethical reflection can be more specifically described as Christian feminist ethics. This can include much of what has already been noted, but also a more direct concern with issues shaped by Christian belief and

theology. Thus, for example, Christian feminist ethics takes a critical stance in relation to past theological justifications of the inferiority of women to men. It opposes the distinction of male and female as polar opposites (representing mind/body, reason/emotion, activity/passivity, dependency/autonomy [sic; autonomy/dependency would seem more consistent]). It challenges the association of women with religious symbols of evil, but it is also opposed to religious "pedestalism," or the expectation that women will be more virtuous than men. A Christian feminist ethics takes seriously the radical feminist critique of Christianity as a religion that can lead to the exaltation of dependence and suffering. As Christian and feminist, then, it takes as one of its tasks the formulation of a theory of moral and religious development and a feminist theory of virtue or character. Christian feminists have also identified problems with traditional concepts of *agape,* and they seek to balance principles of equality and mutuality with the notion of self-sacrifice. Finally, Christian feminists are concerned with the formulation of a theory of justice, one that will illuminate more adequately every form of human and Christian relationship.[4]

I would add that Christian feminists are also concerned to promote equal access to authority and power in the Christian community, and that they ought to make their faith bear on their analyses and critiques of malformations and injustices in the culture at large. In other words, the Christian feminism that I want to promote in this study is radical not in the sense that it wants to isolate women or adopt a lesbian bias, but in the sense that it would combine Christian faith and feminism to criticize (for the sake of healing ills and promoting greater health) all ideas and structures that seem problematic in either the religious or the secular domain. Nothing in the Churches or the other domains of Christian culture is in principle exempt from criticism by ethicists committed to both feminism and the gospel of Christ. And nothing in the secular camps, including the camps of secular feminists, is in principle exempt from a similar criticism. There are no policies or practices so privileged that one cannot ask how they square with the gospel of Christ and/or the proposition (the reality) that women and men are equally human. Full justice in matters of gender is a criterion that Christian feminist ethicists, intent on bringing out what is right, ought to apply always and everywhere.

These Reflections

The reflections on Christian feminist ethics that follow assume a certain relatedness in reality. For example, I am not comfortable separating the moral life from spirituality or doctrinal theology. Indeed, I see each of these concerns as overlapping the other two. For instance, a recent description of the Christian moral life says:

> In the Christian religious tradition, as in the Jewish, morality is markedly religious. That is, it is immediately related to God and its significance is seen in the God-context. It must be so because the Christians view the whole of creation as God's creation and themselves as part of that creation. God is seen as the author and end of it. Everything—morality included—is contextualized and this must in some way be expressed if the Christian's total view of things is to find expression. Morality cannot be regarded as free-standing; in some way it must be described as part of God's purpose or plan.[5]

Similarly holistic is the following description of Christian spirituality:

> Christian spirituality involves the human capacity of self-transcending knowledge, love, and commitment as it is actualized through the experience of God, in Jesus, the Christ, by the gift of the Spirit. Because God's Spirit comes to us only through experience and symbols insep-

arable from human community and history, Christian spirituality includes every dimension of human life.[6]

Finally, note the breadth, the comprehensiveness in this conclusion to a definition of Christian doctrine:

> The function of doctrine within the Christian community is not primarily juridical or legalistic. The primary function of Church teaching, or doctrine, in all the forms it takes, preaching, liturgy, Church pronouncements, the work of theologians, the lives of holy men and women, is to enable each person to appropriate, to internalize, the meaning for the world that God has revealed in Christ. This meaning is dynamic and is understood in relation to the particular concrete circumstances of one's life. Such a task is never-ending. The final word has not been said nor will it be until the end of history.[7]

My desire is to reflect holistically, from the midpoint of a quite traditional Christology, on what Christian feminist ethics has to say about making women, and men, whole, strong, good, holy—in a word, virtuous (fully empowered), without concern for academic boundaries between ethics and theology or ethics and spirituality. I want to examine several concerns that I find prominent in current Christian feminist writings, free of worry that other observers might consign them not to ethics but to theology or spirituality. I want to elaborate ideas about the center of the moral life, the inner self where motions toward evil or good, foolishness or wisdom, tend to lodge, that psychologists and spiritual directors may find as relevant as ethicists. For example, put in the form of questions: How do we best make commitments and keep them? What are the best ways to develop a good, healthy conscience? Christian feminists have done interesting work on these questions recently. I want to comment on some examples of such work as a stimulus to elaborating my own sense of what women know in their bones about commitments and experience.

Similarly, I want to comment on work of Christian feminists that bears on the relations between the sexes, on economic justice, on social justice, even on the imagery we use for God. These are all moral matters, issues that bear on the good life in contrast to the dysfunctional life, the wasted life, the evil life.

As Deuteronomy 30 teaches us unforgettably, the moral way to which God invites us, indeed commands us, is both within our capacity and clear, a product of the radical dichotomy between death and life:

> For this commandment which I command you this day is not too hard for you, neither is it far off. It is not in heaven, that you should say, "Who will go up for us to heaven, and bring it to us, that we may hear it and do it?" Neither is it beyond the sea, that you should say, "Who will go over the sea for us, and bring it to us, that we may hear it and do it?" But the word is very near you; it is in your mouth and in your heart, so that you can do it. See, I have set before you this day life and good, death and evil. ... I call heaven and earth to witness against you this day, that I have set before you life and death, blessing and curse; therefore choose life, that you and your descendants may live, loving the Lord your God, obeying his voice, and cleaving to him (Deut 30:11-15, 19-20).

Reflection, as I understand it, is an effort to estimate the significance of given information—facts, theories, evaluations. Reflection steps back to ponder how given information meshes with other things one knows or other positions one holds. Reflection is therefore concerned with coherence and likelihood. It wants to know how a new singer harmonizes with the chorus already under way. It asks whether a given proposal is likely to promote a fuller disclosure of the truth, or a fuller obedience to the truth, than its competition or its absence. For example, what does a new study of the dynamics of making commitments suggest for our understanding of marital fidelity, or fidelity to God, or the requirements of friendship? What horizon does the study assume, and how does this horizon correspond with the horizon opened by faith in the central significance of the death and resurrection of Christ? How does it cohere with feminist views of women's ways of knowing, or with the mystics' overwhelming conviction that only God can make us faithful or good?

Clearly, a reflective process such as this is never-ending. Its tendency is to begin spinning, from inside a given question, the web of connections necessary to place that question in a fully adequate context. Moreover, the more Christian such a reflective process is, the more it reckons with the divine mystery. The ends of the web pass out of our sight. The more complicated the reflective process becomes, in fidelity to the seemingly infinite complexity of both nature and human meaning, the greater the believer's desire to pivot and move below reflection into the silence of divinity itself.

So, contemplative prayer is a necessary antidote to endless reflection, as well as a proper response to the positive mystery of God, God's being too rich for our comprehension. Contemplative prayer is a movement of health, precious in the measure one feels driven by questioning toward mental illness. Christian contemplation, then, frequently calls a halt, ideally with a wry smile. Again and again, its best yield is the realization that we can never know all that we want to know, even all that we need to know—the realization that we are finite, non-divine.

With such a realization, it becomes clear, at least for the moment, that all moral inquiry ought to proceed by faith. What kind of faith? Certainly Christians will say faith in the divinity revealed in Jesus Christ, but they can also speak of a paradoxical faith in human reason. On the one hand, conscientious reflection finds human reason trustworthy. Allowed to function without pressure or prejudice, our minds do bring us light. On the other hand, human reason easily goes astray because of pressure or prejudice, and it struggles to recognize its limits. This latter point is also paradoxical.

We want to know the totality of our situation, which is God. But we cannot know God as we wish, to the divine essence. We can know that God exists, because we can intuit the need for a complete explanation, a grounding of our knowing and loving, as well as of the physical world. We cannot know what the divine life of knowing and loving, being and creating, is in itself. Our best glimpses are only pale, fragile analogies. God is always more unlike than like what we can know about God, what we can predicate.

All this is elementary, bedrock, traditional Christian conviction, yet ignored by most contemporary ethicists, whether feminist or "male-stream." All this supports thinking hard, and consistently, about striking data or propositions, yet counsels us not to take our reflections too seriously. The most that our reflections can provide is (1) protection against the gross errors of people whose methods are flawed, and (2) orientation to the divine mystery that sets the foundational agenda of all unflawed, rightly ordered consciousnesses.

Even faith in Christ does not protect us completely from subtle errors, and even faith in Christ cannot remove the divine mystery. The incarnation of divine wisdom remains *divine* wisdom, and so something beyond our understanding and control. Christ lets us see enough of the road to distinguish the turns toward death and life, but not the end of the road, where we exit into the mystery of Father, Son, and Spirit. Christ graciously sets us on the path to salvation, but, sinners, we cannot be sure we will not fall off it.

My sense, then, is that these reflections will be successful in the measure that they highlight key issues in the elaboration of a contemporary ethics faithful to both feminism and Christianity, without forgetting or neglecting the divine mystery that is the only adequate context for such issues. What helps us locate the road we ought to walk, the way we ought to proceed into the moral future, is extremely precious, but so is what reminds us that we can never see the end of this road and so must remain humble, that we can never be sure we won't fall off this road and so must double our humility.

The point of balance, as the humble see, lies between rejecting relevant data (for example, those disclosing the injustices women have suffered from men) and drawing from such data unwarranted conclusions (for example, that women ought to hate men). Others can describe the point of balance more elegantly, but perhaps this will suffice. A fateful zone separates what is so from what we ought to do about it. The best Christian ethicists pray their way to a freedom from compulsion, an *apatheia* in the high tradition of the desert masters, that makes their reflections become solid nourishment, for others as well as themselves. Thus I pray that these reflections escape at least my gross biases and feed those readers hungry to know the way to divine life.

❧ 2 ❧

Commitment and Discernment

One interesting and useful way to begin our study of what a contemporary Christian feminist ethics might best stress is to reflect on commitment and discernment, two key factors in the moral life.

Commitment

What ought we to love? To what should we commit ourselves? These questions can epitomize the moral life. Dealing with them clearly and thoroughly assures an ethicist of a respectful, perhaps even an admiring hearing. Margaret Farley has parlayed many years' study of commitment into an admirable book. Consider, for example, what she says of interpersonal commitment:

By explicit, expressed interpersonal commitment I mean promises, contracts, covenants, vows, etc. These commitments provide a prime case for understanding all of the forms of commitment because the elements of commitment appear more clearly in them. We recognize an obligation to act in a certain way within these commitments more frequently than in any others. Moreover, here we most often confront dilemmas and the inescapability of wrenching decisions. It is in these commit-

22

ments that questions of love, of time and change, of competing obligations seem more acute. The very explicitness of promises, or covenants and contracts, places the experience of commitment in bold relief and offers the best chance for understanding it.

There are interpersonal commitments, of course, that are not expressed in any explicit way (at least not in the making of them). For example, some roles that we fill or relationships in which we participate entail commitments, but they become ours without an original choice on our part. We are born into some roles such as daughter or son, sister or brother. Some friendships grow spontaneously and seem to need no promises. Other roles we assume by explicit choice and usually through some external expression—familial roles such as husband or wife, sometimes mother or father, and professional roles like physician or teacher. Even roles we do not at first choose, however, can be understood in great part through understanding the roles we explicitly choose, for roles of whatever kind usually at some points require free and explicit "ratification" or "acceptance."[1]

It is instructive to watch a professional ethicist at work. Typically considerable energy goes into descriptions, distinctions, definitions. In tribute to the complexity of our moral lives, professional ethicists bend over backward to make clear what they are and are not considering. Their worst shame is to appear unsophisticated about the complications, ambiguities, graynesses bedeviling the search for ethical clarity.

So, for example, interpersonal commitments may be divided into explicit and implicit. Explicit may be subdivided into promises, contracts, covenants, vows. Implicit may be subdivided into those stemming from roles we are born into, friendships that seem more spontaneous than chosen, and professional vocations.

The variety of the situations in which we feel responsible to other people, feel as though we owe them debts, is considerable. When we analyze these situations, try to assess our feelings of responsibility, we realize that we are extremely involved. All but the most fleeting or superficial relationships carry obligations. In any significant freely chosen connection to other people, we have "committed" ourselves — sent our pledge that we will honor the agreement, the understanding, explicit or implicit, that we have created in making the connection. In any significant connection that we have not chosen but know exists, we have been committed, perhaps despite ourselves, by the accident of birth, or as a corollary of another, freely chosen commitment, for example, because we have married X, or because we have become a gynecologist.

Clarifying the actual experience of moral realities such as commitments is part of the ethicist's business. We ask those who study ethics professionally to illumine the actual functioning of conscience, the concrete ways that people feel themselves obliged, the various shadings of the conviction that they must be responsible, faithful, because they have made pledges or let others assume they would care for x, y, or z.

Still, Farley's drive to stay close to the full, rich texture of experience seems to me more than standard or merely professional. Reading her work in the context of feminist moral literature as a distinctive bloc, I sense a commitment both generic and personal. Personally, Farley is convinced that ethics doesn't do much good unless it stays close to experience, which is always denser, more complicated, than textbooks suggest. Generically, this is a conviction about which women may feel more strongly than men.

Stereotypically, it is harder for women than men to make simple dichotomies, say yes or no without remainder, accept a rendition of reality wrought in black and white. Actually, most women I know fit this stereotype. By biology and social conditioning both, we feel connected, immersed, and so unable with ease to step back for simple, clear-cut evaluations. Our lives are compromised, because we have grown up to think and feel relationally. It is hard for us to know where we end and our parents, our husbands or lovers, our children begin. When we read Plato, the distinction between soul and body chafes, doesn't wear well. When we read Paul, the deduction of obligatory patterns of behavior from women's and men's disjoint social roles seems simplistic, arbitrary, unrealistic.

Women are the sex of both/and, not either/or. Women are the sex that goes round and round, finds it hard to spit it out, because we know "it" is not simple, that "it" always involves a dozen connections, a half-dozen layers. Women's conversation is often the least important part of a social encounter. What is said is often far less significant than what is felt, sensed, intuited. Women accredit feelings instinctively, automatically, even though, when they are well-educated by either academic institutions or hard knocks, they know the value of letting reflective reason interact with their feelings and restrain them from running wild. All these are generalizations, of course, but ones I make confidently. Even if they do not characterize each woman, experience tells me they do characterize the majority, they are regular if not necessary patterns.

The subtlety of Farley's preferred way of approaching commitments therefore alerts me to the femininity of her intelligence. She is working from a woman's personal angle into the social world, if not from an avowedly feminist angle. But what about the religious, or more specifically Christian aspect of her enterprise? What does she say about the place of faith when it comes to contextualizing a proper study of commitment? She says relatively little, though this little orients her whole book:

> Our experiences in relation to commitment constitute in large part our vantage point for understanding God's commitment to us and God's desire for commitment from us. If God breaks into our lives in a way that shatters the limits of what would otherwise be our experience, this change or expansion of limits becomes part of the experience we must try to understand. Moreover, if by God's gift, God's grace, our experience of commitment is changed, transformed, it is still our experience that must be pondered and in relation to which we must make our choices. The considerations I attempt regarding the "way of fidelity" (and equally so, the way of dis-

cerning when commitments no longer bind) can be considerations of the *way in which grace works* when it works in our lives of commitment. . . .

I assume, therefore, a theological framework, specifically a Christian theological framework, from the beginning. Call it "faith seeking understanding" or call it "thinking about" questions that are so important they press themselves on our minds and hearts. I do not debate doctrines of the human person or of grace or sin or eschatology, though from time to time they appear. But, then, I also do not delineate (let alone justify) the complete ethical theory that is necessary for adequate philosophical support of some of the positions I take. What I do here is partial, and because it requires a whole, it assumes one. I think its requirements are not such, however, that what is here in part will be useless to those whose view as a whole differs in some ways from mine.[2]

This is theology done from the bottom up, a procedure more congenial to Catholics than Protestants. It assumes an analogy between our experiences of human commitment and how commitment works with God. Any revelation useful to us is itself experiential. Even when it ruptures our instinctive categories, the breakthrough is something experiential. Grace is present especially in the peaks and valleys through which commitment walks us. Any time we are involved in something truly significant for our human development, our advance toward greater integrity or our retreat, we may assume that God is interested, involved, a full player in the game. This is the whole that Farley's partial probings of our moral experience assume. This is the overall map on which to locate her surveys of small states of mind and heart.

How significant is it that little reference to Jesus or to Christ appears in Farley's work? What is lost by not providing for the procedure dear to Protestant theology: reasoning from the biblical accounts to human experience? I find myself of two minds. On the one hand, I want to affirm the trustworthiness of "ordinary" human experience, if only because I believe it is extraordinary—always grounded in God's grace. On the other hand, I regret the lack of any explicit confrontation with Jesus or the Christian saints who have best imitated Jesus. So much in ethics depends on one's perspective that not having the most radically Christian perspective available, clearly at work, limits the power of any work on the moral life to shock people with God's otherness and so invite them to a profound conversion.

For example, what do we learn by making Jesus the paradigm of faithful commitment? How ought we to factor in Jesus' extension of the ordinary range of love? Jesus laid down his life for his friends, and for his God. Even if our moral caliber is not that of martyrs, we omit considerations of Jesus' self-sacrificing love at our loss, perhaps even at our peril. What is possible among human beings depends on the models they contemplate, as well as their irremoveable weaknesses. So, my instinct is that a feminist ethics will be Christian in the measure that it allows Jesus Christ (both the historical figure and the risen Lord) the decisive say about what women's well-being entails.[3]

Feminist Friendship

Mary Hunt's feminist theology of friendship challenges this instinct. How can Jesus Christ have the decisive say when much that is associated with Jesus is hard to accept? Specifically, how can the death and resurrection of Christ provide the central paradigm for commitment if it does not match many people's, perhaps especially many women's, understanding of the pledges implied in friendship? Here are Hunt's own words on this topic:

> In fact, women's friendships challenge the adequacy of Christianity's central metaphor, the death and resurrection of a man who laid down his life for his friends. This is one reason why many feminist women find the Christian message so dubious.
>
> Women friends surely would have seen to a woman's

survival and not to her death. Some friends Jesus must have had! Granted friendship does not stop death, but the mystique of giving up life in order to find it again does not appeal as readily to those who are struggling to survive as it might to those who in a "survival of the fittest" contest consider themselves the fittest. A more apt metaphor from women's experience would be the triumph of a group of women over injustice without losing anyone. The mythical dimensions of the resurrection story are decidedly male in this respect. What meaning feminists find in the Christian tradition comes not so much from Jesus and his friends, but from the "Jesus movement," those bonded together in reaction to loss. I can only conclude (in the imaginative constructive mode of Elisabeth Schüssler Fiorenza) that the Jesus movement must have been made up of lots of women just as today's Churches are held together by women's bonds.

Perhaps some of the feminist critique of the artistic rendering of a woman on the cross, "The Crista," is because we intuit that a woman savior would have been significantly different. A more authentic possibility would have been, at the very least, several women killed together for something they believe in. A better image would be a group of women refusing to hand over any one of their own to be killed. Their triumph would be as powerful as any resurrection story to instill hope and sustain memory. How different the Christian tradition would be if either of these were the dominant symbols.[4]

There is much to ponder here. First, the death and resurrection of Jesus (not just any man who laid down his life for his friends) is indeed the central metaphor of Christianity, though one that orthodox Christians have always believed to be fully historical—something that happened in space and time, not just in people's imaginations. Second, it is nice to think that women friends would have seen to the survival of a female savior, but problematic. The gospels themselves agree with Hunt that Jesus had miserable friends. The disciples are portrayed as too slow to understand and too weak to act bravely. However, Jesus had numerous women friends, and they also did not see to his survival. Many women throughout history have had good friends and still not survived horrible deaths—in the Nazi camps and Soviet gulags for instance. Certainly the mystique of giving up life to find it again is problematic; the New Testament Jesus only embraces death because, despite his repugnance, it seems the will (the Lukan "necessity") of his Father.

Is Jesus merely a masochist, or can God's ways contradict our human ones? Is Jesus really acting out a macho fantasy, triumphing in the resurrection as the fittest survivor? There is little evidence of that. Indeed, much in Jesus' behavior, as the gospels report it, runs counter to the stereotypes of male behavior in his day as well as in our own. He challenges any instinctive recourse to violence, he is dubious about all worldly power, and he is certainly not a bully, swaggering and full of himself.

It would also be nice to contemplate a story of salvation worked through a triumph of a group of women over injustice that lost no one, but how would one assure that ending, and would that ending in fact go to the roots of the human condition as effectively as the crucifixion of Christ has done? Fairy tales perform the valuable service of keeping our hopes alive, but a story of salvation faithful to historical realities has to contend with the massive losses that keep occurring. The best of human intentions and efforts often fail to defeat evil, to save even the innocent. And when we do ward off evil for a while, death keeps coming at us. A radical salvation has to defeat death, as well as ward off evil. Christian faith holds that by dying and rising Jesus did defeat death, and did defang evil, once and for all.

The Jesus movement came from the memory, the story of Jesus, and if we can believe the New Testament, the primary accent in that story was not the failure of Jesus but his triumph. After Calvary Jesus was not lost but experienced in a new way. The last chapters of all the gospels, the first chapters of the Acts of the Apostles, and the central chapters of the major epistles of Paul all make this plain. I have no doubt that women played key roles in the establishment of the Church or that without women's genius at bonding the Church would not have survived. But it skews the data badly to suggest that such bonding was a recompense for the loss of Jesus, a kind of keening over the failure of God to effect salvation as women would have wished. The earliest Christian women, like the earliest Christian men, responded to the departure of Jesus in the Spirit of Jesus, who had become for them another Advocate, keeping the memory of Jesus wholly positive.

It is valuable to try to intuit what a woman savior would have been, how she would have announced the reign of God, how God would have re-created the human condition in and through her. It is valuable to imagine how a woman savior might have left Christianity less inclined to exact suffering or the passive acceptance of one's harsh fate. Such exercises free up our imaginations, so that we can understand better the cultural limitations of both the gospels and later Christianity. They allow us to speculate about better ways of expressing the Christian message, ways more likely to appeal to women and give their experience equal weight. Yet the fact remains that Jesus, a male, is the savior-figure from whom Christianity derives (see Luke 2:11; John 4:42; Acts 5:31, 13:23; Eph 5:23; Phil 3:20; 2 Tim 1:10; Titus 1:4, 2:13, 3:6; 2 Pet 1:11, 2:20, 3:18; 1 John 4:14). Thus any serious preferring of a female savior veers toward a rejection of actual Christian faith.

The fact also remains that throughout history women have found Jesus at least as attractive, credible, and effective as a savior as have men. What such women might have thought, felt, or done in other circumstances, if a female savior had been available, is purely speculative. There were goddesses aplenty in the Hellenistic world, all of them symbolizing salvation of some sort, but the women who became Christians preferred Jesus. Nothing much is proved by this fact, but much is cautioned. Mainly, we should be clear that it will be some time, if ever, before the majority of Christian women find imaginary female saviors more adequate than the historical Christ.

Something lovely and heroic appears in the imagery of a

group of women being killed together for a cause, as in the imagery of a group refusing to hand over any one of its own to be killed. But even the gentlest of readers has to note that such a refusal has no guarantee of succeeding, while the theologian, gentle or not, has to note that the real point is what actually happened to make the followers of Christ think that an eschatological salvation had occurred.

Finally, would either story of a group of heroic women in fact be more powerful than the resurrection of Jesus—better able to instill hope and sustain memory? Again, the proposition is so speculative that no one could vote yes or no with any certainty. The only certainty is that, in fact, the death and resurrection of Christ have structured the most powerful story in world history. This is the story that transformed Europe, for weal or woe, and that has also made a huge impact in many other cultures. In claiming to represent actual history, as well as deep psychic processes, the story of Jesus has become the foremost interpretation of how God has dealt with evil. It has made human existence a divine comedy, in Dante's sense. It has made human flesh the conjunction of time and eternity. Because of it, hundreds of millions of human beings have been able to think that their destiny was divinization and eternal bliss.

Naturally, all of these claims and implications of the actual Christian message present problems. None can pass muster before the rationalistic mind. But the twofold criterion of fact and imaginative significance makes the story of Jesus unsurpassed. He actually died and rose. His dying and rising were the definitive transformation of the human condition. That is the traditional Christian faith of the mainstream, laid out in all the creeds, believed by the simple faithful as well as the learned scholars. Is it so impotent today that we should prefer feminist creations not rooted in the history of Jesus and not achieving the radical conquest of sin, death, and finitude?

God is holy, mighty, and immortal. Christ makes his followers holy, mighty, and immortal—participants in God's own being. That has been a faith for which to die, as well as a faith for which to live. It seems almost cruel to compare it with novel tales imagined on the basis of human friendship.

For Christian faith, no human friendship, no matter how tender or fierce, can reach to the marrow of salvation, the extreme of divinization, disclosed by the cross of Christ. Only the grace of God, as uniquely made present by Christ, has such a reach.

For healthy, knowledgeable Christian faith, Jesus is the absolute savior, nonpareil in historical actuality and depth of meaning alike. Certainly there are huge tracts of sinful culture that this faith has yet to raze, abuses against women and homosexuals prominent among them. Certainly the destruction of patriarchy, both outside the Churches and inside, is a monumental imperative. But Christians are bound to believe that the best way to obey this imperative is to appropriate the Spirit of Christ, not try to rewrite divine providence with human quills.

We shall see more of this matter, which soon becomes a question of hermeneutics (how to interpret texts and history, especially in light of past biases), but let me close this section by quoting some ethical remarks of Hunt:

> As lesbian/gay relationships are increasingly visible and accepted, a major issue is what ethical norms will guide such relationships. This is an appropriate question, one that lesbian/gay people ask. It is not enough to say that all is now permissible where nothing used to be allowed. Nor must indiscretions be emphasized as the transition takes place from heterosexism to relational justice. There are simply plenty of new ethical questions to ask and plenty of new people asking them. This is what it means to be involved in a spiral process where one answer leads to new questions and questioners.
>
> What about age differences, multiple partners, casual sexual encounters? Old models that condemn homosexuality out of hand are not helpful here. But neither is it fair to leave a large segment of the population without moral anchors, indeed to leave everyone with the impression that there are no lesbian/gay sexual ethical parameters. That there are, and that they may differ from and influence the existing ones based on hetero-

sexual relationships, is something that will come about only by trying on or experimenting with various approaches.[5]

I believe that the crucial Christian ethical norm is love, that responsible experimenting balances docility to past wisdom with freedom to hear new wisdom from Christ's Spirit today, and that heterosexuals ought to listen to what lesbians and gays say about their moral struggles more than preach to them norms based on heterosexuality. There is a great mystery about all sexuality, as about all love. The first rule of a prudent, truly faith-filled ethics is to attend reverently to what God seems to be doing in a given situation—to where a given course of action seems in fact to be carrying the people following it. If that is what Hunt believes, as seems possible, perhaps even probable, I agree with her ethically, despite our differences concerning the place of Jesus.

Feminist Biblical Hermeneutics

Mary Hunt quoted Elisabeth Schüssler Fiorenza in support of her imaginative construction of the place of women in the Jesus movement. I find Schüssler Fiorenza's general view of feminist hermeneutics stimulating:

A feminist critical hermeneutics of liberation seeks to read the Bible in the context of believing communities of women, of the "Church of women." It realizes that a feminist re-vision and transformation of biblical history and community can only be achieved through a critical evaluation of patriarchal biblical history and androcentric texts. It recognizes, as a hermeneutic feminist principle, that being woman and being Christian is a social, historical, and cultural ecclesial process. ... A feminist "politics and ethics of scriptural remembrance" that shapes the Christian community as a community of moral discourse must keep alive the sufferings and hopes of biblical women and other "subordinate" peoples in order to change and transform the patriarchal structures and ideologies of the Christian Churches shaped by the New Testament pattern of patriarchal submission and silence. In the final analysis a critical feminist hermeneutics of the Bible must call patriarchal biblical religion to personal and structural conversion of feminist praxis before it can proclaim that the communities shaped by the Scriptures are the "community of the forgiven."[6]

A critical hermeneutics is a theory of interpretation based on rational analysis rather than credulity. It is feminist when it promotes the equality of women to men in humanity, liberationist when it promotes the freedom of any oppressed group. It is Christian when Jesus Christ stands at its center, offering the decisive paradigm of how God wants human nature to be. For such a hermeneutics to read the Bible in the context of "believing communities of women" requires an act of imagination, since it must try to find those communities in the early Christian centuries. Inasmuch as it tries to find those communities nowadays, such a hermeneutics requires an act of faith that the Spirit of Christ is inspiring groups of faithful women, giving them wisdom and strength for the entire Christian Church.

The "Church of women" that I can support is not a coven closed to men, but the entire body of Jesus' followers, to the extent that it makes women the full equals of men. In addition, I can endorse ad hoc assemblies, mainly if not exclusively of Christian women, that support women's struggles to claim such equality, and groups of whatever composition that focus on the oppression of women to learn how the gospel of Christ would have us liberate all oppressed people.

If we are to take biblical history to heart so that it liberates all oppressed people, for whom in the present instance women can stand special duty, we have to deal with that history critically. Specifically, we have to locate and analyze the patriarchal portions, the texts that make male humanity the norm for humanity at large, and (I would add) the deviations in the history of biblical interpretation that have exacerbated women's oppressions. Moreover, the actual reality of either one's female personhood or one's Christian faith is not something timeless but a reality set in the cross-hairs of historical, social, cultural, and ecclesial forces. The community of Christ exists in time, continuing to suffer all the shapings by time to which its Master was subject.

In the measure that it preaches the full humanity of Jesus, the complete entry of the Word of God into human flesh, the community of Christ ought to preach the full humanity of Christ's followers, with the noteworthy addition that, unlike their Master, these followers have been sinners. Whether one's hermeneutics is concerned with the biblical period or later historical periods, it should imagine the lives of women to be varied and much shaped by the specific ethical traditions of their given cultures. If it fails to exercise such an imagination, a hermeneutics is not fully incarnational and so not fully Christian.

A feminist politics and ethics of scriptural remembrance lives by a liberated imagination of the biblical past. To shape the Christian community toward a moral discourse, an ongoing ethical conversation worthy of its Master, it has to deal with Scripture not as fixed to traditional meanings, especially patriarchal ones, but as a compound of divine revelation that cannot fail and historically conditioned, fully human, and occasionally sinful assumptions, practices, and ways of thinking. A great stimulus to keep approaching biblical texts freshly, with the demand that they yield their truly saving significance in the present, is to remember regularly the sufferings of women portrayed in the Bible; women past and present who have clung to the Bible for support in their struggles to love God, their neighbours, and themselves; and other people who have suffered in a biblical context.

The best target for this remembering, the clearest enemy of liberation on which to focus, is bound for feminists to be the patriarchal aspects of the Christian Churches, both those represented in the New Testament and those that through history have looked to the New Testament for guidance. Patriarchy, the exaltation of men over women, has infected the structures of all the Christian Churches, from the beginnings indicated by the New Testament itself. It infected the structures created by Jesus, in reflection of his Jewish culture, reminding us that even if we confess the sinlessness of Jesus we cannot pluck him out of a sinful environment, cannot confess that all his interactions with that environment resulted in sinless structures for his community.

The same is true of what Schüssler Fiorenza calls "ideologies," patterns of thought, more or less consciously self-promoting. The pattern we find in the New Testament of asking women to be subject to men and of keeping silent about the radical equality of women with men (which equality ought to have led to the complete practical parity of women in all aspects of Church life) must come under scrutiny, if need be under attack, because it was both wrong in itself (incompatible with the liberation Jesus wanted to effect) and the source of widespread, often compounded later wrongs.

So, finally, the hermeneutics I want to champion asks patriarchal biblical religion for conversion. In light of the marriage of feminism and the gospel, such a hermeneutics claims that biblical ideas and practices are inauthentic when they denigrate women in any way. Inasmuch as feminism means rescuing women from denigration, from inequality, biblical religionists must be feminists, and actively so. Not to act for any oppressed group is to sanction its continued oppression. Without such a conversion, no Christians can rightly call themselves forgiven. They cannot promote their assemblies as communities of those whom God has pardoned and made whole, because there are sins of which they have yet to repent.

Glossed in this way I find Schüssler Fiorenza's hermeneutical stance congenial. I cannot endorse any truly separatist organization or ideology. For the bedrock issues most central to faith, women and men always hold more in common than apart. But when apprized of the sexist biases of much biblical religion, any Christians whom I can admire will repent and refocus their belief in the gospel. I note that, perhaps unlike Hunt, Schüssler Fiorenza does not despair of the power of the gospel to liberate women, and all other oppressed people. I locate such a hope in the perception that Jesus has accomplished the essentials of salvation, regardless of the painful ways in which we continue to discover how much is not yet saved in practice.

I believe that, ultimately, only a high Christology, one confessing the strict divinity of Jesus as the divine Word made flesh, can anchor this hope. It is not something that historical evidence can certify, though there are on the historical record enough instances of salvation taking hold of individuals, and even of a few communities, to make Christian claims for salvation worth hearing somewhat docilely.

One ought to add that no interpreter, no matter how well equipped with the latest in critical tools or feminist insight, stands apart as a sinless, wholly objective and unbiased exegete. One also ought to add that it is unchristian to expect absolute purity in history, and so to postpone one's acceptance of Jesus and/or his Church to the day when it has been proved that all has been made well in practice. The eschatological dimension of Christian faith is not only a promise that a victory won in principle will flower fully when God chooses to bring history to its climax. It is also a caution not to leap out of one's skin and overlook the deficiencies, the sins, that have dogged every group known to history, including the earliest Christians.

This does not mean that we should dismiss efforts such as women-Church to form Christian communities dedicated to liberating women by the power of the gospel. It does mean that we should not imagine such communities will be sinless or without their own problems, including, for example, women's problems of loving men as their brothers, accepting the actual conditions of a sinful history, and accepting the legitimacy of the historical "Great Church," despite its actual sins, such as sexism, and its inevitable deficiencies. If we do not reckon with the sinfulness of all human ventures, we become utopian in a pejorative sense, gnostic in ways incompatible with an orthodox, healthy Christian wisdom.

Discerning Jesus' Feminine Vision

For ten years Rosemary Haughton has labored with homeless women in Gloucester, Massachusetts, trying to provide

them shelter, food, and the chance to recoup so that they can
learn how to survive in the world of work, and the chance to
heal their battered spirits (and often their battered bodies as
well). Haughton sees Wellspring House, the enterprise with
which she is involved, as a miniature of the works necessary
to redeem careless, stupid societies from the vices and policies
that are ruining the lives of so many people, most promi-
nently poor women. A truly radical, prophetic Christianity
moves in her own wellsprings, giving warm, vulnerable flesh
to the more theoretical interpretations of the gospel's liberating power that scholars such as Schüssler Fiorenza pro-
pound.

Consider, for example, Haughton's sense of the vision of
the Israelite prophets and Jesus:

> Basically, the vision of the prophets and of Jesus was a
> "right brain," feminine understanding of human life.
> This is why the Church which tried to carry on his work
> so soon lost touch with his vision, in a world where the
> feminine was despised. This is why the whole of later
> Western culture, built on ideals of total control of nature
> and of lesser human beings, has driven into exile those
> insights and skills which Jesus perceived as central to
> the establishment of the reign of God, and which the
> women around him grasped — if not fully, at least
> deeply.
>
> The reign of God that Jesus proclaimed is not vague
> or impractical. It is an earthy and earthly job of making
> the planet a place where human beings can be at home
> with each other and with God. Jesus spent a great deal
> of his time and energy defending his vision against peo-
> ple who couldn't or wouldn't understand it — most of his
> parables were addressed to his critics and opponents —
> and in the end it was only in his death that the thing he
> lived in and for could enter deeply enough into the con-
> sciousness of humanity to become invulnerable to death.
> Because of his willingness to let go his earlier hopes and
> yet never to let go the reality which was his whole being,
> he carried with him into the very heart of the human

mystery the elusive yet enduring knowledge that God's sons and daughters can actually live as such in the home which is God's earth.[7]

In this sketch of Jesus' vision, the enemy is control—the effort to dominate nature and lesser human beings. Haughton does not in this text probe the source of this effort to gain dominance. It seems clear that insecurity—lack of faith in the goodness of the mysteries of creation and being human—is a good candidate. Not believing that God will be God, people try to take on the attributes of God. That is idolatry, and it is bound to fail. We cannot control nature like autocrats, self-proclaimed gods, because we cannot understand nature to its depths. We have to let nature instruct us how to live with it well, for the mutual flourishing of all species.

Similarly, we cannot control being human autocratically, as though it were our dominion, because we cannot understand being human to its depths. Our minds are limited, and our own depths are roiled. We have to invite people to reveal themselves to us, show us their needs and potential contributions. The insights and skills that Jesus perceived to be central to establishing the reign of God in our midst went in this direction. Jesus knew from his own union with God that God's ways are only persuasive, never coercive. All God's ways are ways of love. We may never understand how they can be so, and we will never be able to replicate them fully, but that is what Jesus knew them to be, and his knowledge was therapeutic. He could touch people, heal people, draw people out of their fears, their insecurities, because the finger of God had anointed his own brow. Led by the Spirit, he could create communities of friends, sisters and brothers, because he could show them the joy of living outside their anxious selves, in the love of God that fashioned their best centers.

Haughton loves to contemplate the earthiness of this creative work. Jesus did not hie off to a monastery. He did not tell people to despise their bodies or shun their work. He stayed in the midst of his people, teaching and healing them. He cast out demons and fought the forces opposed to God's reign, the causes of so much human suffering. He blessed food and drink, marital love, the friendship of men and women, all efforts to succor the poor, the outcast, the despised, the supposedly sinful. Haughton's great desire is to find the planet a humane habitat. She longs for people to feel at home with one another and God. Wellspring does not have clients but guests. It seeks what Christian monasteries have long sought by committing themselves to hospitality: the provision of welcome, acceptance, friendship, practical help. It wants to be, in all modesty, a sign that the planet could be hospitable, if we would shift our gaze, reform our vision, free up our hearts.

Inasmuch as a desire such as this derives from Jesus and contemplates the model he has provided, it is well equipped to deal with the sufferings of trying to live hospitably and to oppose or reform all that makes the planet inhospitable. The cross of Christ is inseparable from his earthly work of incarnating the love of God. But from the cross of Christ, Haughton sees, came a power stronger than human unbelief, fear, unwillingness to give up deadly controls, reluctance to live hospitably. However one estimates the exemplary sufferings of Christ, the adequacy of Christ as a real-metaphor of human pathos, one has to acknowledge that the Crucified has forced Western cultures, indeed all people who contemplate him seriously, to ask themselves for what they should be willing to die.

If Jesus' laying down his life for his friends produced so unforgettable a portrait of humanity, so indelible a model of holy love, serious people must compare their own estimates of how to live well, what to treasure and what to despise, with those broadcast from the cross. Relatedly, any serious people must ponder the resurrection of Jesus, which put the seal of divine approval on his way of the cross. Together, the two phases of Jesus' consummation did indeed make his vision, right-brained and feminine, invulnerable to death. His vision was so intertwined with spiritual life, with intellectual honesty and sacramental love, that it came to mind whenever people familiar with Christian iconography wanted to cure the sicknesses malforming humanity and serve the full flourishing of human beings in health, vitality, joy and peace.

Haughton's concluding sentence takes us to the edge of a defensible Christian utopianism. By being willing to let the will of his God take him to abandonment and death, Jesus went into the heart of the human mystery, where the divine obscurity becomes the foremost reality, carrying his desires, his hopes for healing human beings and making the planet hospitable, to their source, the divine creative love that could secure them — make them more real than everything that seemed to crush them. The fate of Jesus is the one lesson people have to take to heart, if they are to know how to live as sons and daughters of God in the home which is God's earth.

Jesus won, triumphed, was proven right. The light shone in the darkness, and the darkness never overcame it. That has remained true down the two thousand years separating us from Jesus, and it remains true today. Jesus' vision of human friendship and a hospitable earth continues to inspire enough people to make God's reality, even God's name, a powerful contender in the battle for people's hearts. The freedom that Jesus showed, his ability to commit his entire being into God's keeping and so make his entire being available to other human beings, has no serious competitors. When it comes to powers able to make human beings human, Haughton finds the vision, the Spirit of Jesus, nonpareil.

Moreover, as Schüssler Fiorenza rightly requires, the freedom that his Father gave Jesus, that Jesus enjoyed as the birthright of a heavenly Son come into space and time, was exquisitely historical, actual, human. In dialectical support of the freedom that Haughton senses the guests of Wellspring most need, the freedom of Jesus becomes the healthy utopia, the eminently real "no-place" that shows us how to make our present places fit to live in, homey, welcoming, congenial to the best of our desires and needs, the best of our generosities and loves.

Most of the women who live at Wellspring as guests are not familiar with traditional Christian symbols, have not taken them to heart through years of participating in the Christian liturgy. Yet the staff of Wellspring has felt the need to celebrate high times such as Holy Week and to invite all the guests to participate. In describing what happened at one Easter Vigil, Haughton paints a dramatic picture of how the miracle does happen occasionally, the house does become a home redolent of heaven, God's home that fulfills our earthiness:

The lights all over the house were turned off, leaving one room for those who didn't want to attend. We were preparing to go outside and light a new fire in an old iron cauldron. Suddenly the separation seemed unbearable. Nancy went to the women and asked them to join us—please come—at least try. So they came, nervous, giggling a little, polite but not too pleased. The fire was lighted, and blessed, the candle lit, the chant rose, the light spread, carrying candles through the dark house, lighting every candle we could find, coming at last to the dark chapel. The big white candle stood among flowers, the chant of the "Exultet" (ancient and strange and just right) blessed the rising of light out of the darkness. It was Marygrace who sang it, coming back with her husband to share with us the time of rebirth.

The women listened, looked at each other, a little apart, wondering. There were the readings, commenting, telling, celebrating, bringing into our time the proclamation of victory over death. And the blessing of the water. It shimmered in a big dish before the table on which the candle burned. Water of cleansing, of birthing. Two by two, we came forward and blessed each other with the newly blessed water; one of the community touched a guest seated beside her, beckoned her forward. They touched each other with the water. Then two guests came together, then another community member and two more guests, in a laughing trio. One girl, bug eyed, sat and watched but did not move. Nancy came to her, her hands still wet, touched her with the water and kissed her, the girl's face broke into a smile. Suddenly, we were not two groups, but one. The great symbols worked. It all came together. The room was filled with a sense of power and conviction; you couldn't pin it down, it doesn't last, in a sense, and yet it is real, it happened, it is remembered.[8]

Surely this is one text that needs no ethical gloss.

Discerning Love

God is love. Christians inherit this article of faith from the Johannine literature of the New Testament. Ethicists committed to the New Testament have to reckon with love throughout their analyses. Love bears on the motivation, goal, and substance of any human action. With what feelings does the person initiate the action? What relation to the other people involved does the person want to achieve? How does the person conduct the process of the action? In an ideal action, a Christian ethicist finds love prominent in all phases, and so finds intimations of God.

Feminists can be leery of love. If justice is lacking, love can seem the better that is the enemy of the good. First let there be justice, equity, fair-dealing, however envisioned or constrained. First let there be equal pay for women, equal health care, equal access to power and service in the Churches. Then we can speak about ideals such as loving one another into full prosperity, treating one another with a selflessness that might symbolize a completely good God.

In fact, though, we seldom get justice without love. Love is always challenging our assumptions about justice, fidelity, commitments, discernments of what is good and what evil, what compatible with Christ's way and what incompatible. Perhaps it will advance our reflections, and place them back in touch with the real lives of people like Anna, the woman with whom we began, to contemplate the virtues of another well-wrought literary figure, the mother and main voice in Jane Smiley's gripping novella *Ordinary Love*.

The woman's twenty-five-year-old twins are reuniting, meeting again in the family home that all the children have both left and not left. The twins, boys, have been apart for several years. So the return of one from a tour with the Peace

Corps in India has the whole household on edge. The mother is divorced. Her husband, brilliant but difficult, has receded to the edge of her consciousness, though he is still powerful in her memory. As she watches the family reunion unfold, she shows the reader how the different members have gotten to their present stations, especially she herself. The children blame their father for the divorce, which came after he spirited them away to England. They don't know that their mother's affair with a neighbor precipitated his actions. They also don't know how thoroughly their father humiliated her for her infidelity, reducing her to poverty of both body and spirit: a low-paying job, a soul desperate for not seeing them. Eventually the children shuttled back and forth between the parents, but the novella depends on the differences between the children's views of the past and their mother's.

During the reunion, when the now-adult children's problems begin to tumble out, the mother finds herself, against all expectation, telling them about her affair. In the course of her narrative, she repeats insights into desire that have become key to her self-understanding. Her oldest child, a daughter who has always been competitive with her, pushes her to explain a grin or grimace she gave when learning about the daughter's marital troubles. Here is how Smiley describes the woman talking to herself, as she prepares to answer her daughter:

> I can say something general—about desire, maybe, about how if a person wants something enough there is always room for it. She knows I think desire is the only motivation. Or I could make up a story about someone at work, some woman with a job and a bunch of kids and a husband and a lover on the side. She goes without lunch, she goes without noon-time aerobics, she picks up her kids half an hour later at the day-care center. She is rigidly alert, the way I was. I could make her live, make them laugh at her. . . . She's dressed a little better every day than she used to be, wearing a little more makeup, so focused and attentive that her work is not only always done, her desk is always neat. She straight-

ens it compulsively, doesn't she? A new life is coursing through her unlike any previous life—this time she is married, and what she feels is compounded equally of terror and desire. I could say she knows what I know but didn't know twenty years ago, that both the terror and the desire will be fulfilled.[9]

Later, speaking frankly of the affair, the woman says:

It felt most like some fixed, inconsolable longing. It was constant, even when I was at his place. I would go over there, and it would stop the moment I saw him, but only that moment. After that there was so much that he was holding back from me that I was as filled with longing when I was with him as when I wasn't. After we made love, he would sleep and I would lie there wondering what you kids were doing at camp and nursery school. . . . My experience is that you make room for anything you want, if you want it enough. Even an inconvenient man.[10]

What does all this suggest about feminism, Christianity, and ethics? A great deal. First, the woman has been a traditional homemaker, married to a brilliant man who expected her to serve him and manage his children. She was not traditional, however, in having desires of her own that she would not, or could not, subordinate to him. Without her knowing it, expecting it, her longing for connection, love, became so strong that an affair with a romantic but completely unsuitable man occurred. It more happened to her than stemmed from her free choices. But while it was occurring, she let nothing get in its way. Call it longing or love or some inseparable mixture, it possessed her. She would rearrange her entire life to make it keep happening. It did not disrupt her work or her care for her children, but it did shift everything else in her life to the periphery. It ended after her husband took the children away. Her lover wouldn't even see her, as though she'd become contagious, polluted. It took her a year to get over him, and she will bear the scars of the affair for the rest of her life. She has had no fully satisfying relations with men since. But while it occurred it riveted her whole being. In retrospect, she wonders if anything since has ever satisfied her, even as she realizes that the affair certainly did not. Now she lives for small satisfactions, not the least seeing her children develop tangled lives of their own and watching her grandchildren line up to follow them.

So, the woman calls to mind many stereotypes in which feminists trade. At the decisive time when she had the affair, she needed a center, and she did not know where to find it. Her talents were under-utilized, and she had no fulfilling connection, no love that tied her into contentment. She was only half aware that her behavior, especially her affair, was a cry for help. She felt her longing through and through, but she had no friends to help her understand it, no fellow women with whom to talk it through.

In older age, at the time she tells her story, she has gained a certain integrity, but it is more solitary than most women would like. She has good, though complicated relations with her children, but none with her peers. Her life suggests the price of maturing in a pre-feminist time. Her actions were admirable, inasmuch as she tried to assert herself and find love. But they were also destructive, perhaps deliberately so. She wanted to punish her husband for his inattention and selfishness, but she also wanted to punish herself—for being what she did not want to be. So she interpreted her longing and the unhappiness it revealed to her as right to bring her great pain. Her world has become that of a stoic: unhappiness is sure to come; we can only prepare to endure it. A feminist philosophy of life, based on connections to other women, would have served her much better. That is how many feminists would reason.

Christians are bound to note the religious vacuum at the center of the woman's life. She has no God and apparently feels no need for one. She has no tradition to instruct her in either expectable states of soul or right and wrong, wisdom and foolishness. She is intelligent, so she learns from her mistakes, but often she reinvents the wheel. She has no community to support her in suffering, no public liturgy that deals with desire and grace. No tradition of prayer instructs her about enlightenment and forgiveness, about how to address the mystery at the center of her being and open herself to its ministrations.

So she seems culturally bereft. Her schooling, formal and informal, has not prepared her to cope with spiritual crises. She has been taught little about love, the heart of the human matter. Had she been dealing with Jesus, his Father, their Spirit, she would have learned lessons for her peace. One can't give assurances that these lessons would have saved her from bad mistakes, but one can say that they might have redirected her longing. That is how committed Christians would tend to respond to the woman's story.

In Christian ethical perspective, our deepest longings are for God. They never leave us completely, but from time to time the grace of God stops them, soothes them, promises that one day all will be well. This grace helps us bear our burdens. Opening ourselves to it, we can manage to meet most of our responsibilities, fulfill most of our commitments. We can even manage to put up with our selves, so imperfect and demanding. If we are mature, we don't seek God's grace, God's touch, in order to cope with our lives. We seek God for God's own sake. But we are not ashamed to present our needs to God, because God has invited us to do so. Finding that God, sought for God's own sake, loves the whole of our selves and lives, we can even make God a partner to our crucial decisions, such as those about our human loves, both the honest ones and the illicit.

This brings us to the ethical crunch. The narrator has done wrong, bringing disaster on herself and her children. But her wrong was part of a whole pattern of wrongs, many of them done to her. She should have calculated better the likely impact of her longings and loves, but that is hard to do when one is captive to them. She should not have been captive to them, but who of us is wholly free? She would do well to repent of her mistakes, especially when she glimpses the harm they have done her children. Perhaps much in her solitude, her minimalism, amounts to repentance. Not having a living God, she has done well to survive with some integrity. She does not excuse herself for her mistakes, though she still does not understand how they happened. She does not pity herself. She sees her pain as the price of self-knowledge, and she finds it acceptable. She wishes things had turned out otherwise, but she can accept what has come to be.

In assessing the woman's state of mind when she entered the illicit affair, what she did, what happened to her, and how she now regards the past, the feminist Christian ethicist has to grant her much respect. She has violated important objective norms, and she has been untrue to some of her own convictions, but she did not intend evil, she has borne the consequences of her misdeeds, and she does not curse God. We should not blame society for her adultery or for its bad effects on her children, but we have to include society (the cultural milieu), her husband, and her lover when we apportion blame.

Finally, we have to confess the limits of our ethical evaluations. We cannot read the woman's heart, cannot know the depths of her loves, any more than she herself can. The story of her life, structured by her adultery, remains patent only to God. What we can say only touches the surface. Even as we warn others not to go and do likewise, we have to note that her actions had some good consequences. She broke free of an oppressive husband. She came to appreciate her need for her children, and so to treat them well when reunited with them. And she came to think little of herself in a good sense, gaining a salutary humility. All these good consequences might mean that God wrote something straight with crooked lines. Certainly a Christian feminist ethics has to hope so.

ᦵ 3 ᦵ

Social Ethics

The Feminist Voice

In an impressive critique of Pope John Paul II's encyclical *Sollicitudo Rei Socialis* (1987), which deals with social ethics, Maria Riley has concluded:

> *Sollicitudo Rei Socialis* is an important but dated document. Its failure resides in its blindness to the essential contribution that feminists, both women and men, are making to the development debate. I suggest that the framers and consultants of this document are trapped by the myopic position that "women's issues" are marginal to the so-called great issues of our day. This particular myopia results from a patriarchal mind-set. Mainline development theory and practice has also been shaped by patriarchal thinking. Ironically, it has been the very failure of that development over the last few decades that has opened the way among some groups to reassess the development process from women's perspectives. It is becoming clearer that "women's issues" are not marginal; they are central to the search for the kind of development in which people matter. *Sollicitudo Rei Socialis* would have been enriched by the voices and insights of women.[1]

What are some of the insights of women that Riley has in mind? First, that any fully useful and truly humane assessment of development policies has to take into account not only gross figures on economic production, agricultural production, the military sector, banking transactions, and the like, but also matters of microeconomics—for example, how households of poor people are managing. For instance, if the International Monetary Fund, in demanding changes in the economic policies of debtor nations before granting them loans, requires cuts in public expenditures for health care, housing, education, water, utilities, and the upkeep of roads, the effects on poor households (where women and children predominate) can be devastating.

The same with the devaluation of currency. Women can find their meager resources stretched even farther and more claims made on their time (because they have to fill in new gaps caused by the retraction of social services). The other side of this coin is that people wanting to know how the poor actually survive in wretched circumstances ought to study the creativity that women develop. By networking, finding new sources of income, and finding new ways to save income, women the world over make it possible for poor households to keep going. However minimal the levels of food, shelter, clothing, education, health care, and the rest that the poor manage to achieve, without the creativity of women things would be much worse.

For example, one of the central causes of widespread hunger in Africa has been policies that have taken away women's traditional role as subsistence farmers charged with the task of feeding their families. When government policies have shifted from subsistence plots to communal farms aimed at raising cash crops for export, they have often taken women out of the agricultural loop and left them no land to farm. Without land to farm, the women have not been able to supply the staple, minimal levels of food on which their families, indeed their whole cultures, have long depended. Makers of such policies might be well-intentioned, but their neglect of how traditional economies have actually functioned, especially concerning the obligations and contributions of women, has resulted in disastrous mistakes.

Another oversight in the present policies of people responsible for the development of poor nations is the neglect of the link between the education of women and population control. Not only do women on the whole earn money in proportion to their levels of education, they also limit their families in the same proportion. With more education, women also tend to care for the health of their children more effectively, learning more about the sicknesses likely to afflict the children and the programs available for their care.

In many traditionally poor countries the education of women has been a low priority. Available educational opportunities have gone mainly to men. Certainly men continue to need better education, but often the assumption has been that the public orientation of men's education—its focus on matters of science, technology, and business—would best cure the people's poverty. Looking more privately at how families actually function spotlights the crucial role of women. For example, begetting children and caring for them has at least as much to do with the future of a developing country, including its future economic status, as learning about Western business practices. Thus, educational policies that do not help women understand their poverty, learn how to limit their families, and care for their children can leave poor countries little changed.

The pope's encyclical urged a new spirit of solidarity that might break down conflicts between the First and Second Worlds, to the benefit of poor people in the Third and Fourth Worlds. From Riley's feminist perspective, the best way to bring this about is to stress the mutuality that recent theoretical work has underscored:

> But if relationships are to express true solidarity, they must be built on mutuality. *Sollicitudo Rei Socialis* condemns the relationships of domination that presently rule our world, particularly in the "desire for profit . . . and the thirst for power" (no. 37). . . . Feminism identifies this will to dominate as part of the culture of patri-

archy. Mutuality in relationship is the feminist alternative to domination. Mutuality moves beyond equality
to recognize the reciprocity of giving and receiving, caring and being cared for. In its negative expression, it
recognizes the reciprocity of evil, of harming and being
harmed, of hating and being hateful. Solidarity, without
mutuality, easily slips into paternalism or maternalism.[2]

The implications of this feminist stress on mutuality include
rethinking such problems as racism and sexism. The racist
suffers along with the victim of racism. The racist, too, is
diminished in spirit, in human substance. The twisted relationship is a two-way street. The evil carries a destructive
mutuality. The same with the relationship between the person
expressing sexist biases and the person suffering from them.
Riley is not saying there is no distinction between sinner and
sinned against. She is not equating the two effects of the sin.
But she is reminding us that both the perpetrator and the
victim are affected. The situation belongs to neither of them
exclusively. The two are in it together, for woe. The bad
effects are mutual.

Feminists would have a new stress on mutuality, along with
a new respect for the place of women in all questions of social
justice, and would revamp our going social ethics. Whether
in the Churches or outside, the going models are not so thoroughly mutualistic as reality itself tends to be. Relatedly, they
are not so sensitive to the effects of given policies on women,
or the reactions of women in accepting or rejecting such policies, as they have to be if they are to promote positive effects.

For Christian ethicists, the neglect of women's roles, voices,
interests, and sufferings in many Church documents and
many Church policies is a simple matter of patriarchal bias.
The Churches are too little different from the cultures in
which they exist. They are too little formed to prophetic distinction. Where they ought to take the social stance of the
Israelite prophets and Jesus to heart, assuming a preferential
option for the marginalized, they tend to concentrate on the
reform of mainstream institutions. Yet, in their official statements many of the Churches have taken a preferential option

for the poor. Many have noted the negative effects of mainstream institutions and policies on women and children. But much more remains to be done.

As the encyclical *Sollicitudo Rei Socialis* suggests, the concerns and insights of women have yet to become structural in papal policy. Women have yet to be invited into the precincts where Roman Catholic social thought is formulated. The reason is less a deliberate desire to exclude women than a lack of any sense that it is necessary, even urgent, to include women. That lack, that unawareness, is typical of how a relatively benevolent, well-intentioned patriarchy tends to operate. It simply assumes that it knows what is good for women, as well as for men, because it assumes that it knows what human nature requires always and everywhere. Human nature, as represented by the patriarchal leaders themselves, is ready to hand, patent for all to examine. The fact that women are not ready to hand, are not represented at the tables where the documents are hammered out, is seldom noted.

I conclude from analyses such as Riley's that Christian social ethicists would do well to insist as a matter of fundamental methodology that women have a voice equal to that of men. One way to do this is by requesting equal numbers of women, equal representation, but the numbers are less important than the conviction that women's voice is crucial. Until the day when an appreciation of the radically dual sexuality of human nature has led to the realization that women ought to shape social policies as influentially as men, we shall continue to suffer from myopic, one-sided, and so ineffectual public policies. The differences of women from men, which flow from both the different bodies (and so psyches) that women inhabit and the different social roles that they tend to assume, ensure that policies not fashioned with a full contribution from women will be unreasonable. How that full contribution of women comes about is relatively unimportant. That it come about ought to absorb all Christian feminists.

In the Churches it would be an act of virtue to submit all significant social statements and policies (or, perhaps better, all policies of all kinds) to the analysis of knowledgeable women. It would empower the Churches by opening them to further sources of insight, and it would make amends for the past neglect of women's voices. I do not think that women ought to have a power of veto over such statements and policies. I would not want women's voices to be the final say. Rather, my sense is that a proper mutuality would mean an ongoing conversation between women and men about all statements and policies of interest to both. With mutual respect, those drafting Church policies ought to be able to incorporate the reactions of all the groups that the policies would affect significantly. (In principle, then, I would argue that all minority voices ought to be solicited, not just those of women.) Granted the right atmosphere, it ought then to be possible to locate the areas of concern, suffering, and sense that are truly common—shared by both the have-nots and the haves.

But what is this right atmosphere? It is precisely the difference between Christian ethical ventures and those of people without Christian faith: a sense of mutuality rooted in the commitment of all parties to Jesus the Christ. In light of that commitment, the divine life that is the goal of all human striving comes as a gift from God. No sex, racial group, age group, ethnic group, or other segment of the human family has special claims on it or privileged wisdom about it.

Perhaps the elderly, having more experience, ought to have the first word, but the young, being less routinized, also ought to speak up and be heard. Perhaps men, having more experience of exercising overt Church power, ought to speak first about practicalities, but women, having less loyalty to the status quo, also ought to point out how past policies have failed the simple faithful.

For example, if a Church's social or sexual ethical policies are not winning the support of the poor, or women, or young people, women aware of this failure ought to speak out boldly. Indeed, the sexes always need to listen to one another, lest they equate the whole with their own partiality. So the right atmosphere for truly Christian ethics is the presence of Christ's Spirit, who for faith alone makes the whole realistic.

Economic Justice

Development usually refers to the overall improvement of poor countries. Although the first indexes that analysts use may be economic, health and education are also implied. The same holds when we contemplate social issues in the United States. The linchpin is economic justice: the right to earn a fair wage. But rights to health care and education are always implied. This means that statistics on poverty are merely the tip of the iceberg. When we contemplate the lives of Americans living below the poverty level (established by overly benign government criteria), we have to multiply the sufferings entailed. People who lose their jobs, or can earn only the minimum wage, tend to be less well educated and more prone to sickness than people who can earn a decent living. The children of poor people suffer numerous cultural disadvantages, not simply less adequate food, shelter, and schooling. Christian ethicists therefore urge us to let ourselves *see* the effects of economic policies that increase the ranks of the poor. Feminist ethicists urge us to let ourselves see how many of the poor are women and children.

These exhortations combine in several telling paragraphs from an article by Joan Walsh that surveyed the national scene at the end of the 1980s:

> The most disturbing feature of modern American life that the religious economic justice statements seek to address is the persistent number of people living in poverty. After following a steady downward curve from the mid-1960s through the 1970s, poverty rates arched upward in the 1980s. There were 4.3 million more Americans who fell into poverty between 1979 and 1985 alone, and most of them were women and children. As the U.S. Catholic bishops note, "We are the first industrialized nation in the world in which children are the poorest age group." One out of four American children under the age of six lives below the poverty line today.
>
> Cutbacks in welfare eligibility, which pushed 557,000

people off the public assistance rolls in the early 1980s, were one culprit in rising poverty rates. Reagan administration spending cuts hit programs for low income Americans twice as hard as other social programs.

Yet increasingly in the 1980s, the "poor" are not just the clients of public welfare agencies, but workers supporting families on low-wage jobs. Between 1978 and 1986, the number of adults working at least thirty hours a week but still living in poverty jumped fifty-two percent, to include seven million Americans — more than a third of all poor adults in the U.S., and twice the number of adults receiving Aid to Families with Dependent Children, for instance. Others who make up the "new poor" have worked their whole lifetimes, only to be thrown out of work in plant closures, layoffs and shutdowns.[3]

This situation only worsened under the Bush administration, especially during the recession of 1991-92.

Unsophisticated critics of the Reagan administration tended to call the increase of poverty scandalous and blame it on greed. Because of the personal example, as well as the public policies of President and Mrs. Reagan, the poor had lost their traditional claim on the consciences of the wealthy, to the great shame of the wealthy. The relaxation of governmental concern for justice had allowed the entrepreneurs and lawyers to wax fat with no worries about the social effects of their practices. Led by glittery, gilded leaders in the White House, American culture had thrown off the restraints inherited from its Puritan forebears and exulted in high living, ostentation, and conspicuous consumption. Greed was good. Let the poor eat cake.

I am one of those unsophisticates. Whenever I read complicated analyses of how our national economy has turned away from manufacturing and agriculture to the provision of "services," I keep waiting to learn why this should increase the numbers of the poor. Whenever I read analyses of trading in junk bonds or arranging leveraged buy-outs, I keep waiting to learn how this benefits the country at large. I'm still waiting. So I have concluded that the root of the problem is religious: a loss of soul. The people moving our economy away from the common good, toward greater benefits for the rich and greater neglect of children and others who are especially vulnerable, have no moral health in them. They are blind to the proper functions of business and government, which are to promote prosperity and peace for the entire citizenry. They have become so disordered that they are leading our country into a valley of cultural death, where the sufferings of the marginalized are sure to foment revolutions, more or less violent. Consider, for example, the riots in Los Angeles in the spring of 1992.

It is no rebuttal to say that socialism of the Soviet and Eastern European varieties has failed miserably. That does not make capitalism sacred. One of the best aspects of the social writings of Pope John Paul II has been an evenhanded analysis of the failures of both the Communist and the capitalist systems. Certainly the liberal traditions of most of the capitalist countries have kept them from violating human rights as egregiously as the Communist nations have done, but capitalism itself is seldom compatible with the gospel of Christ.

The usual horizon in which a capitalist economy works has no place for the gospel's imperatives to render justice to the poor. It rejects the teaching of the Church fathers that no one has the right to luxuries so long as anyone lacks necessities. For Jesus, the goods of the earth existed for all the earth's people. In creating, God spread out the bounty of nature for the entirety of the human race. All human beings were made in the image and likeness of God. For the evangelists and Church fathers, Christ had died for all. Thus for some people to accumulate much more than they needed while others starved was a deeply sinful disorder. For a national economy to pay more attention to interest rates and stock prices than to the number of children suffering in poverty would reveal a mortal sickness of soul.

Is this merely religious rhetoric, or does it bear ethical truths? The reader will have to say. I believe, though, that it expresses what most Christian feminists concerned with the morality of U.S. economic policies feel in their bones. The

disorders are profound. The goals set by those policies are
blinkered, and bound to be so, because they are targeted by
leaders both self-centered and self-serving. Lobbyists for large
corporations and the interests of the wealthy have much
greater clout than advocates for the poor. The needs of people of color, ethnic minorities, women, and children matter
far less than the wants of white males. The large corporations
and the military have a larger claim on those guiding the
economy than do people on welfare. The need to dominate
has more influence than the need to consult, cooperate, col-
laborate. Women's instinct that economic reality, like all other
realities, is relational, mutual, makes little impact. At best,
fairness, economic justice, is conceived as a level playing field.
Usually we do not achieve even that. Usually we not only
neglect all those unequipped to play the game, as it is presently defined, but we also tilt things in favor of the current
titleholders.

None of this economic skewedness is compatible with a
Christian reading of reality or a feminist reading of the gospel. All of it reeks of original sin, compounded by frequent
personal sins of greed. The practical neglect of children and
the poor cries to God for redress. The selfishness and neglect
of the common good remind any prophetic Christian of the
blindnesses that God visits on the corrupt soul for its condem-
nation. Thus both feminist and Christian ethical programs
are bound to appear counter-cultural. Granted the current
bias of the U.S. economy against seeing the goods of the earth
as given by God for all the earth's people, current U.S. economic policies ought regularly to feel the lash of task forces
in the Churches and synagogues.

Perhaps things have always been thus. Certainly the U.S.
is not the only disordered nation in history. Nonetheless, no
one desiring to follow Christ or render to the poor (the majority of whom are women and children) a justice equal to that
enjoyed by the rich (the majority of whom are men) can
accept current U.S. policies. Any feminist Christians of moral
sensitivity have to deplore the current statistics on poverty,
homelessness, unemployment, and such related matters as
drug addiction and crime, seeing them as expressions of sin-

ful closure to God. Indeed, to claim to be either Christian or feminist and not deplore them, not turn one's core spirit against the false values from which they spring, is to land oneself with the scribes and Pharisees, the hypocrites against whom Jesus lashed out in hot anger.

If Christian feminist ethicists wanted a single economic trend on which to focus their analyses, Walsh would probably suggest the shift to a service economy. The results of this shift have been dramatic, and only by reevaluating it, with an eye to paying people working in the service sector not what the market will bear but what their families require, can Christian feminist ethicists stand tall:

> Significantly, the economic justice statements of the religious community don't isolate the poor, but place them on a continuum of national economic insecurity brought about by profound economic shifts, most notably the nation's transition from a manufacturing to a service and information economy. In its statement *Christian Faith and Economic Life*, the United Church of Christ points to the 11.5 million industrial workers who lost their jobs between 1979 and 1984. Of five million surveyed in 1986, a third were still unemployed, and almost half of those with new jobs took substantial pay cuts.
>
> The shift from a manufacturing to a service economy has changed the nature and expectations of employment in the U.S., perhaps permanently. Wrote the Catholic bishops: "By 1990, service industries are expected to employ seventy-two percent of the labor force. Much of the job growth in the 1980s is expected to be in traditionally low-paying, high-turnover jobs such as sales, clerical, janitorial and food service. Too often these jobs do not have career ladders leading to higher skilled, higher paying jobs. Thus, the changing industrial and occupational mix in the U.S. economy could result in a shift toward lower paying and lower skilled jobs."[4]

Clearly, the only way to keep this shift from being an economic disaster is to change the criteria according to which jobs are recompensed.

A New Biblical Hermeneutic

When she considers how Christian ethicists ought to picture their method in light of such injustices as inequitable salaries, Karen Lebacqz joins the camp of the liberation theologians:

> A new hermeneutic is needed. Biblical remembrance itself requires historical consciousness. Scripture is read through the eyes of those who are oppressed: "theology must start with the horizontal plane, with people where they are and how they live." The starting point both for theology and for exegesis and textual interpretation is the lived experience of those who struggle against oceans of injustice. As Dorothee Sölle puts it, "Bible texts are best read with a pair of glasses made out of today's newspaper."
>
> The goal of biblical remembrance is not understanding of the text but a new and liberating praxis. Here we move toward a new method for approaching justice.
>
> How do we know that women's role is rape, that the gap between rich and poor is robbery, and that description is rhetoric? We know it because that is the way it is perceived and understood by those who are the victims of the system. We know it because we the oppressed live it. "Those who benefit from social injustice are naturally less capable of understanding its real character than those who suffer from it . . . ." These prophetic words of Reinhold Niebuhr, spoken so many decades ago, are echoed by liberation theologians today: "Being poor, we are closer to reality than whose who are in the center, in the money." There is an "epistemological privilege" to the position and perspectives of the poor and oppressed.[5]

First, Lebacqz feels the need to outflank the fundamentalist wing of biblical interpretation, which takes a literal mind to the Bible and often ends up endorsing injustices. Certainly a literal mind is better than complete neglect of the Bible, because even the brute text of the prophets and Jesus makes it clear that one cannot serve both God and mammon. On the other hand, the Bible stems from patriarchal cultures. Both testaments are limited by the horizons of their human authors. Certainly much in the Bible works against these limitations, as though the authors often wrote (often were inspired by God to write) better than they realized. But limitations such as a tolerance of slavery and the second-class status of women remain. Inasmuch as they hinder the prosecution of the justice that the biblical God manifestly requires, one must deny them in the name of the Bible's own more central message.

Admittedly this raises the question of a canon within the canon of biblical texts. But the proper answer to this question is neither to forbid ethical criticism of any canonical text nor to take certain "ideologically unacceptable" texts out of circulation. It is to enter into the hermeneutical circle, in which the Bible challenges the reader and the reader challenges the Bible, with complete honesty. It is to brave the Bible's threats to our myopia even as we tax certain biblical texts with biases of their own.

Second, in the spirit of Jesus preaching the Sermon on the Mount, blessing the poor and others freed by their marginal cultural status or their moral eccentricity to embrace the Kingdom of God, Lebacqz moves to make the poor the privileged interpreters of the biblical message. Inasmuch as the gospel, for instance, is a message of liberation, calling oppressors to desist from their oppression and the oppressed to seize the liberty of the children of God, it resounds most powerfully in the poor, the oppressed, the marginalized, the outcast— those most in need of liberation. If Jesus is the sun of justice, coming to shine a new light for those whose subjection to powers of darkness had threatened to take away their hope, then those in thrall to injustice are most likely to note his dawning, appreciate his warmth, understand how his light has revealed a new set of possibilities.

The quotation from Dorothee Sölle, reminiscent of Karl Barth, sets up a dialectical relationship between the Bible and current events. If the Bible casts a fresh light on current events, one to which secular analysts are often blind, current events cast a fresh light on the Bible. Whether Croatians struggling for independence in Yugoslavia, or blacks struggling for freedom in South Africa, or little people struggling for recompense for losses inflicted by corrupt managers of Savings and Loan institutions, the stories we find in the newspaper spell out what the gospel has to mean if it is to be good news for present-day men and women: justice, hope.

Third, what Lebacqz calls "biblical remembrance" is the dangerous imagery associated with Jesus, who turned worldly values upside down. To her mind, the point to healthy Christian biblical interpretation is not arid, purely academic understanding of the text but insight into the liberating behavior that the text both clarifies and empowers. Reflecting on the string of illustrations that she offers creates solid hypotheses about her message. The subordinate role assigned to women in patriarchal readings of the Bible (in concert with the Bible's own patriarchal biases) amounts to rape: violence against women's proper autonomy and integrity. The gap between rich and poor that one can witness in today's world gets no sanction from a proper, defensible interpretation of the Bible. It is straight robbery, because the goods of the earth belong to all the earth's people—there ought to be no great chasm between the fortunate and the unfortunate. And those who stick to the level of description, telling us only what probably went on at the surface of Jesus' activity or the activity of the Israelite prophets, are mere rhetoricians—people playing with words rather than realities, truths, imperatives from God. Unless interpreters descend to the level of conversion, repentance from sinful practices and embrace of just ones, they more alienate us from the Bible than help us into its God-given power.

These are the perceptions, the convictions, of the people who read the Bible with the urgency of sore need. Take a person unemployed, discriminated against because of sex or color, trying to get medical treatment without an insurance card. This person is on the outs with the going system. She has learned, in her heart of hearts, that the going system is unjust; it denies her humanity, her basically equal standing with all other human beings. By the accident of having lost her job, or being Asian, or not being eligible (by criteria largely determined by the profit motive) for insurance, she has become a non-person, someone whose cries for help can be ignored. How can she believe in a God who sanctions such a system? She cannot, so she repudiates any reading of the Bible that props up the unjust status quo. She says that a genuine word of God would give her the good news that God not only supports her desires for just, humane, kindly treatment, but that God also condemns the systems stacked against her. They are no work of God. They are idols, built by greed and unbelief.

So, fourth, Lebacqz is ready to grant the poor an epistemological privilege. If you want to understand reality as biblical revelation discloses it to be, you have to enter into the interpretational viewpoint of those most needing the liberation entailed in that revelation. You cannot know the justice of God from a position of privilege within an unjust system. You cannot be an oppressor and grasp the power of God's word to free those oppressed. That is the either/or entailed in Jesus' preaching. Those who are not with him are against him, because those who are not with him are siding with injustice. They are closing themselves to the call of God announcing a new arrangement of human affairs. Henceforth the great goods will not be riches, power, sources of prideful self-esteem. Henceforth the great goods will be availability to God, service of one's neighbor, the humble realization that everything belongs to God and only comes to human beings by grace.

In extension of Lebacqz's liberational stance on biblical interpretation and ethics, I would make only two further points. First, it might be clearer that God retains complete sovereignty over the faithful interpreter, as well as over the process of salvation history. We cannot pontificate about what *has* to be in the history of salvation. In the measure that we know God, we realize that all priority and control have to remain with the divinity. No matter how powerful a liberational hermeneutic may seem, it cannot dictate to God the terms on which salvation can occur. That is the valid insight of conservatives who often oppose liberation theology, though probably few liberation theologians would deny it. God is always greater than our theories of justice. God has ways of rendering justice to the poor more profound and ingenious than we can imagine.

Second, some impatient liberation theologians need to hear the refrain of the Bible that in patience we shall possess our souls. They need to take to heart the elementary reality that even they are the pots, not the potter. God is sovereignly free, or God is not God. Not even liberation theology, close to the poorest of God's suffering people, can dictate to God the times or ways of liberation. Certainly it is possible to think that God wants us to storm heaven and demand a quick visitation of divine justice. Certainly Abraham praying for Sodom and Job contesting with God remain instructive paradigms of honest prayer. But balancing this is the foundational word of Jesus, the human stance of the Word itself come into time: Your will be done.

We do not dictate to God the times or the ways of salvation. Our entire lives depend on God's grace. God is not beholden to us in any way, and no ideology of ours can capture God. We become idolaters if we think that it does. We forget the elementary facts of our finitude, mortality, and sinfulness. God is the Creator. God is the Savior. We are unprofitable servants, even in our most successful hours. Liberation theology has to take these simple truths to heart and make sure its righteous impatience, its ardent desire for speedy justice to help the poor, does not neglect the bedrock fact that the gospel means what God wants it to mean. The gospel is the aboriginal truth, far more primordial than any human truth such as liberation theology. All Christians have to believe that this is so, so all Christians have to walk humbly before their God and not put words in their God's mouth.

Anti-Semitism

One of the most painful lessons for feminist ethicists has come from the discovery that a commitment to the equality

of women with men does not automatically erase other prejudices. One can see clearly the injustices done to women yet
not see clearly the injustices done to blacks, Jews, Asians, or
other minorities. Within the feminist ranks, women have had
to confront their own presuppositions and prejudices. They
have had to realize that being female is not the only occasion
of suffering discrimination. Black women have taxed white
women with a racism little different from that shown by white
men. Jewish women have taxed Christian women with an
anti-Semitism little different from that of Christian men. Less
frequent is the self-criticism that would lead black women to
tax themselves with prejudices against whites, or that would
lead Jewish women to tax themselves with prejudices against
Christians, but perhaps in the next, more mature phase of
feminist ethics we shall see more of such mutuality.

To be more concrete, let us consider the case of anti-Semitism. Judith Plaskow has described well some of the burdens
she, and no doubt most other sensitive Jews, suffered from
the unthinking assumptions of a Midwestern culture that
amalgamated Americanism and Christianity:

When I lived in Wichita, Kansas, the local newspaper
had a big picture of a sunrise on its cover one Easter
with a caption remarking on how the coming of Easter
brings a smile to the face of everyone, whether or not
they are Christian. Such blithe cultural imperialism
masks not only the indifference of most of the world
toward Easter but also the Jewish historical experience
of Easter as a time of fear, a time when Christians could
be expected to take revenge on their Jewish neighbors
for the death of Christ. This cultural imperialism is part
of a broader phenomenon that shapes the experience
of every oppressed group: the oppressed must know the
oppressor's culture, but the oppressor need know nothing about the oppressed. Ironic as this is given the Jewish roots of Christianity, American Jews necessarily
acquire a surface knowledge of major Christian beliefs
and celebrations, while particularly outside of New York

City, Christians are often totally ignorant of Jewish holy days and their meaning.[6]

This is a valid description of both Wichita in particular and U.S. culture in general. Protestant Christians, especially, equate Americanism with Christianity and expect that Christmas and Easter will be received as American holidays. Most Christians know little about the traditions of non-Christians, and often they care less. How profound an anti-Semitism this involves is another question. It involves ignorance, certainly, and a bias in favor of Christianity. It involves the Christian assumption that Judaism is an antique, a relic pushed to the historical margins by the new and definitive thing done by God in Christ. But much of it is simply the self-interest of a majority group not sophisticated enough or good enough to look beyond its own borders. Unfortunately, that phenomenon is not limited to Christian Americans.

Saying this implies no approval of Christian myopia, no defense of anti-Semitism. It is only the foundation for an appeal for more self-criticism on the part of minority groups claiming prejudice against them. It only is the beginning of a hope that all groups will become quicker to acknowledge their own forms of insularity and prejudice. Plaskow's *Standing Again at Sinai: Judaism from a Feminist Perspective*[7] deals well with Jewish prejudices against women, and it is not afraid to criticize Israel's treatment of Palestinians. However, it does not sound the waters of Jewish biases against Christians.

My experience is that any realistic assessment of anti-Semitism, like any realistic assessment of racism and sexism, has to reckon frankly with the sinfulness of the oppressed as well as the oppressors. I do not mean that we should equate the two sinfulnesses. I am not offering the oppressors any escape from their serious sins. For example, the fact that my victims are imperfect does not excuse me for injuring them. But acknowledging the imperfection of all parties does introduce a note of realism sometimes lacking in the accounts that victims offer. It does remove any claim, seldom explicit but often tacit, to absolute innocence.

Thus, one of the further questions that one has to ask of

liberational ethical stances like Lebacqz's is when the epistemological privilege of the poor ceases and one has to factor
in the sins of the poor, their own blindnesses, hatreds, prejudices, closures to God. Similarly, one of the further questions
that one has to ask those complaining of anti-Semitism or
racism or sexism is how their own consciences, or those of the
group for whom they are speaking, stand. Do they see no
sinful prejudice of Jews against Christians, of blacks against
whites, of women against men?

Common sense, ordinary experience, simple honesty in the
examination of one's own conscience says they should. Why
not acknowledge it? Why not place more nuance on the status
of the victim and admit that one can't be sure how things
would have worked out had one's own kind been in the driv-
er's seat? When I hear such acknowledgments, I feel a surge
of hope. Perhaps, just perhaps, this ecumenical group, this
grievance committee, wants to deal with the full truth, not
just political positions. Perhaps this will actually be a group
submitting itself to the judgment of God and emerging with
all members transformed. This hope, I admit, is a deduction
from a Christian anthropology. I believe, in virtue of my faith
as much as my experience, that all people are blinkered, limited, sinful. I have yet to find a group, Christian or non-
Christian, that does not tend to favor its own kind and depre-
ciate outsiders.

I would have Christian ethicists take the lead in champi-
oning the rights of political and religious minorities and urging their fellow Christians to esteem the religious traditions
of their non-Christian neighbors. But I cannot be surprised
that many Christians remain sinfully indifferent, for my sense
is that all peoples are slow to move outside their own religious
and ethnic ghettoes. Indeed, sometimes I find Christian ethicists excessive in their efforts to accommodate to non-Christians. Sometimes dubious feelings of guilt exert an irrational
influence. The Holocaust and the history of American racism
are realities giving Christians many grounds for reforming
their past practices and ideas. But when one finds Christians
born after 1960 beating their breasts in guilt it's time to ask
a few further questions. For example, are such Christians dis-

tinguishing between longstanding traditions of anti-Semitism
or racism over which they had no control and current sins of
anti-Semitism or racism which they can control—which they
must repudiate, if they are to maintain a good conscience?
Are they distinguishing between the operation of original sin,
which is not personal, and evil free choices which very much
are?

Certainly, the too-guilty Christian ethicist is not the only
kind, probably not the majority kind. Often Christian ethicists, like the constituencies they are trying to serve, can be
insular, prejudiced, slow to see their own biases and repent
of them. But does this make Christian ethicists different from
other groups? Are Jewish, black, or feminist ethicists ipso
facto more insightful or virtuous, let alone the constituencies
they are trying to reach?

Here, then, is a nice question. How does the epistemological privilege of the poor actually work out? It is clear, I think,
that "the poor," the marginalized, those who suffer discrimination are more aware than "the rich" of the injustices that
given cultural patterns create. Because their oxen are gored,
the poor are quicker to realize that certain policies are wrongheaded. But is the behavior of the poor necessarily virtuous?
Are they bound to follow the Suffering Servant of Isaiah and
make the injustice done them redemptive? I find the answer
to this question less clear.

Certainly some of the poor realize that to gore the oxen of
others would be equally wrong, but some poor people under-
standably do not look beyond their own pains, cannot stop
craving vengeance, do not learn the lesson of Isaiah. Suffering
is only ennobling when it takes people beyond the law of the
jungle. Only when people see that tit for tat never brings
redemption, can never bring about radical change of the
human condition for the better, can one say that being victimized has brought them to wisdom. This is Christ's very high,
demanding standard: love your enemies, do good to those
who persecute you.

Thus women who come into power and do not treat well
those they can abuse blunt the personal significance of the
sexism they have suffered. As well, such women render moot

any putative epistemological privilege. The same is true for other minority groups. God abhors all ill-treatment, but God makes ill-treatment that occasions self-criticism, wisdom, and a purer love redemptive. The poor have to let God work through their hateful sufferings if they are to become the betters of the rich—those who know better, love better, are better in the sight of God.

This is not an ethical position likely to go down well in any of the minority camps. Yet I do not see how a Christian ethicist can avoid this conclusion. After one has charged the majority groups, those with the greatest power, with the major responsibility for what goes wrong, what becomes unjust in a given culture, one has to honor the equal humanity of the minority groups by suggesting that they too may bear some responsibility. Thus I am most edified by, am happiest with, any minority group—female, black, Jewish, whatever—when it not only complains about victimhood, mistreatment by others, but also shows itself self-critical, anxious to root out its own sins, confess them, and repent of how it has victimized others.

This is parallel to how I am most edified by the leaders of my Roman Catholic community. I would be more impressed by the social teachings of Pope John Paul II and the Vatican if, in addition to preaching to the world, they took the imperatives of the gospel to heart publicly and repented of the Church's own many and grievous sins throughout history— not the least those against women, Jews, blacks, and other children of God living as religious or cultural minorities. Indeed, I have stopped listening to Church leaders who do not make their own failings as prominent as the failings of those they are castigating. Why? Because I know that I am as liable to prejudice as any man who has denigrated me because I am a woman, any person of another color who has categorized me impersonally because I am white, any non-Catholic who has written me off because of my Irish-Catholic heritage, any non-Christian or unbeliever who has scoffed at my efforts to be a decent academic, intellectual citizen of the twentieth century, calling that impossible for a believer. I have learned that I should spend at least as much time examining my own conscience as passing judgment on people different from me.

Black Feminism

Toinette M. Eugene's essay "While Love Is Unfashionable" describes the union of spirituality and sexuality in traditional black culture, then draws the consequences for black feminism:

> Black feminism as a concept is *not* meant to describe militant, manhating females who are strict separatists without sensitivity for anyone but themselves—a sort of chauvinism in reverse. Black feminism is defined as a self-acceptance, satisfaction, and security of black women within themselves. Similarly, in the case of black men who understand themselves as feminists, black feminism for them is an attitude of acceptance of black women as peers—an attitude which is verifiable in their behavior and efforts on behalf of and in solidarity with black women. Black feminism proceeds from the understanding, acceptance, and affirmation of black women as equal and mutual in relation to black men, to an increasing openness of mind and heart to be in solidarity with and in self-sacrificing compassion and action for others who have also been oppressed or marginal in society. This solidarity includes being in communion and consultation with all Third World peoples, and implies dialogue and discussion with white women's liberation actions as well as with gay liberation movements in this country.[8]

Eugene has previously shown the holism of native African views of spirituality and sexuality. She has also shown the debilitating effects of slavery, which swung a wrecking ball into traditional African family patterns and caused great distrust between black men and women. Now she is concerned with how black women might grow into greater self-posses-

sion, greater enjoyment of their bodies, and better response
to the desires of their spirits for holiness. Counseled by the
faith of the black Christian Church, she senses that the spirituality she seeks can set no artificial boundaries. In principle,
it must be universal, a love that tries to imitate the God who
makes the rain to fall and the sun to shine on just and unjust
alike.

This is a crucial ethical insight. Christian religion ought to
follow Jesus in his unrestricted love. Christ reached out to his
God, who was goodness without limitation. He reached out
to all people in need. No one was Christ's enemy. Anyone
could be Christ's friend. Those who did become Christ's enemies choose to be such. They rejected him; he did not reject
them. So Eugene can only come from the black Church to
feminism with a large heart. She cannot conceive of black
feminist spirituality as something separatist, parochial, self-
limiting. To do that would be to deny Christ, her master, to
deny God, who gives divine life without limitation.

The psychological beginnings of a healthy black feminism
boil down to self-acceptance, self-love. If any of us are to love
our neighbors as ourselves, we'd best love ourselves well. To
be engaged in a reverse chauvinism would contradict the
healthy origins of black feminism. People who accept themselves, who find themselves acceptable in God's sight, have
no need to hate others. They have little instinct to reject the
other sex, or other economic classes, or other races, or other
religions. If God has so loved them, they ought to love one
another—all other human beings, who are equally children
of God.

The satisfaction and security that black feminism requires
lodge in the depths of black women's souls. When black
women are content with themselves, confident that, whatever
their material circumstances, their lives remain lovely gifts of
God, they are not likely to fall into destructive emotions,
whether of self-hatred or hatred of others. When they feel
secure in God, well-connected to the ground of creation and
the Redeemer of humankind, they have little temptation to
see other people as threats and so lash out at them, launch
preemptive strikes. The fact that many black women have

approached this ideal while living in terrible poverty speaks volumes for both their faith and the power of God.

The ideal that Eugene imagines has black women and men sharing these convictions. When black men and women think of themselves as equals, comrades in their struggles for fuller liberation, they break down the many barriers that history and sin have conspired to raise between them. The solidarity of black women and men makes it easier for both to feel compassionate toward others who have suffered social injustices. It breeds an openness to other cultures, other realms of experience. Black women feeling confident about their own identity, comfortable with their own liberation movement, can engage sympathetically with white feminists, third-world peoples, gays and lesbians, any group feeling the pinch of oppression and trying to free itself.

In this mood Eugene suggests why the fulfillment of ethics comes from faith, hope, and love—virtues fostered in the interactions with divinity that constitute a living religion. If ethical action is the doing of what is right, the full achievement of ethical action comes from a reformation of human character such that it knows what is right innately and does it joyously. Such knowledge comes from living with who or what is to be known. For example, spouses in a good marriage tend to develop an intuitive understanding of what the other most deeply wants, most characteristically says and does, at core finally is. Holy people enjoy a connatural understanding of God. Through years of prayer and study, they take on the mind of Christ, or the inner pulse of the Torah, or the passionate submission to God that sings in the Qur'an. The faith, hope, and love that fulfill the agenda of Christian feminist ethicists are powers derived from openness to God. They come to term when the Holy Spirit takes over the person's deepest identity, so that she or he abides in God's own love. From this abiding passion flows the strength to do what is right, say what is fitting, render justice to all people.

It is only by faith in God, for instance, that a black feminist such as Eugene can be certain that she should enter circles of mutuality with men. Nothing purely empirical can prove that openness to men will do her more good than harm, bring her more insight than grief. Relatedly, it is only by hope that she can keep going to meetings with white feminists, confident that her efforts will bear fruit, her time and energy will not have been wasted. When we are in the proper spiritual groove, faith and hope allow us to find a third dimension in all our analyses, commitments, experiences, accomplishments. Nothing is merely itself. Everything suggests a drawing by God, a lift of its deepest being toward its goal, which is also its source.

But the greatest of the theological virtues is love. Eugene still believes in love, hopes in love, gambles on love. She still thinks it worthwhile to try to love all other people, especially fellow sufferers. When she can feel the love of God, she knows that a given friendship or project is right and just. Love justifies any decent relationship, because God is love. Love is unfashionable nowadays, because it is so easy to be cynical.

But there is a love that can never hurt, that is always self-justifying. That is the love poured forth in our hearts by the Holy Spirit (Rom 5:5), which is pure grace. That is the love Eugene is looking for. That is the source of the black feminism she desires. The simple, obligatory Christian deduction is that because human beings are made for God, who is love, our fulfillment through human interactions is paid out in love. All the better that black religious traditions tend to make this love earthy, joyous, opposed to any dichotomizing of flesh and spirit. All the better that Christian black feminists can look to the Incarnation to justify their desire to keep love enfleshed, fully real, a thing of nerves, bones, history, community.

These instincts make black feminist Christian spirituality a virtual paradigm for the quests that all women, and feminist men, are facing at present. In Rosemary Haughton's terms, the new holy grail is a decent way to feel at home in God's world. Black feminist Christian spirituality of Eugene's kind offers a suggestive model for how to find this grail. When we embrace ourselves as gifts of God, and keep our love of other people, indeed of all other creatures, unrestricted, we come into a stunning liberation.

Latin American Accents

From the underside of history the poor women of Africa, Asia, and Latin America fight to do what is right. Even in the most trying circumstances most of them struggle to protect their children, hold their families together, endure their sufferings without cursing God. Consuela del Prado, writing about women from the barrios of Peru, catches the nobility of such women's struggles:

Women of the poorer sectors suffer and weep much over their situation. They live in an estranged world. They are torn from their land; they are deprived of their schools, their language, and their traditional clothing as well as their children, spouses, and their place in the community. If poverty is death then poor women confront many deaths in their lifetime: the death from hunger, sickness, repression, the death of their tradition, and of their deepest femininity.

One day while I was attending a neighborhood celebration of the Senor de los Milagros (the Lord of Miracles) in Lima, I heard the beautiful prayer of a woman asking the Lord for health and life for her family members, for the orphans and widows of the country, and especially for those who lived in the area of Ayachucho where there is so much pain and death. The woman, in spite of her own suffering, was aware of the pain of others. She felt called to give up her individualism for the community.

There are many women in the poor sectors who, like this woman, go from their own experience of poverty and need to serve the community, often through their commitment to organizations set up to help others. Living this way gives them a new sense of the God of Life because it demands that they give up their individualism for the good of the community where they feel they are worth something and their lives and experiences are appreciated. This is what is meant by the living God's call to life in abundance.[9]

To begin from the end, I must note that life in abundance is good life, ethical life, life as the mores and promises of one's people have said it could be. Everywhere, people's traditions have oriented them toward this life. Everywhere, the function of tradition, myth, ritual has been to make the good life, the life of "our" ethos (customs, way of being human) attractive. The living God's call to this life sounds through the community. The Scriptures, traditional teachings, ceremonies, and even bare being of the community itself testify to what the people's God asks of it, what the people's God invites it to. This God is no God unless living. For the people of Lima, God might as well not be, unless God can do something about poverty and other forms of suffering. Christianity might as well vacate the wretched scene if it has no power to transform the scene.

The idea that even the poor have to sacrifice their individualism for the community, and that the community is where the poor can find the appreciation they need to keep going, goes to the center of Latin American liberation theology and ethics. In part this reflects the Latin American peoples' own traditions, which remain free of the individualism that has flourished in the modern Western industrialized nations. In part it reflects a (related) reading of the gospel. People are members of one body, the Body of Christ. They only intensify their sufferings if they remain isolated, whether in spirit or in body. Until they set their lives in the context of their community, their lives are not properly focused.

So, even to pray for others is an act of solidarity, realism, and liberation. Just to let one's spirit transcend one's own sufferings, on the way to caring for the sufferings of others, offers a chance to overcome the loneliness that suffering can inflict. This chance is more than the dismal consolation of realizing that others are in the same wretched straits as oneself. It goes to the heart of the Christian conception of human existence. None of us lives or dies alone. Whether we realize it or not, we share a common condition. Others in our neighborhood, our generation, are going through much the same painful passage as we. Whenever we acknowledge them, reach out to comfort them, we forge bonds that somewhat ease our common passage.

This instinct is stereotypically feminine. Women are the ones who draw the chairs into a circle, so that each person can see the faces of the others. Women are the ones who instinctively form networks, because their children are thrown together in school, in neighborhood games, even in jeopardy from sickness or crime. As though the connection between mother and child forged in the womb has stamped the feminine character through and through, women are seldom comfortable with separation, seldom hell-bent for autonomy. Women want to cooperate rather than compete. We know that we are all in it (this business of making the world a fit place to live) together, so it is mere common sense for us to cooperate.

This knowledge includes realizing our need to cooperate against death. The "it" in which we live, move, and have our being is mortal. Certainly we can hope that the immortal God secures our global milieu at a level below death. But our passage to our God takes us through death. Poverty anticipates death, adumbrates death, because it destroys so many hopes. The poor woman who had hoped for a happy family life sees her hopes die, because she can barely get enough food to feed her family, because her children are ill-clad, because her husband and sons are forced into wretched toil, or warfare, or general depression. Traditions die, because cultural sickness comes over them as surely as physical sickness comes over the elderly or the malnourished young. People feel uprooted, threatened with meaninglessness. They no longer know who they are, because they have become nobodies, casual casualties of inhumane, ungodly forces that seem to roll over them as though they were bugs.

No wonder poor people hunger for community. No wonder religious people working in the barrios have tried to make the local Churches part and parcel of the people's life. And no wonder that Mary, the Mother of God, becomes Mary, the Mother of the Poor. As a recent study of the place of Marian piety in the grassroots or base communities of Latin America puts it:

> The base communities are prophetic Church, taking shape in the midst of conflicts. These small groups of people who are poor and unimportant, who take their inspiration from the gospels, disturb the powerful, and they are defamed and calumniated by some, while others envy them and want to manipulate them. In the midst of these interwoven conflicts, the base communities keep trying to cut out their own path and always regain their bearings from their fidelity to the God of life who has called them and brought them together. In a similar manner, conflict was always latent throughout Mary's whole experience, as the gospels narrate it. She went through a "different" and unique kind of gestation and gave birth in the midst of the strains created by the Roman occupation force, far from her own land and relatives, an exile and uprooted with her newborn son. She was a follower of this same son in his project of forging a Kingdom, and then her son fell out of favor with the religious and civil authorities of that period, and she became the mother of the one sentenced and crucified. Thus Mary represents the people faithful to God, bearing oppression and persecution so the Light may shine and liberation may become reality. It is in the heart of that dialectical tension between anguish and hope, between love and suffering, that Mary and the people of the base communities lift their prophetic cry to denounce injustice and announce the liberation that has already taken place, and is now taking place for those who hope in Yahweh.[10]

Mary, the person who knew great conflict, saw great suffering, had her soul pierced by the fate of her child, is not only a model for many suffering Latin American women but also a type of the Church standing by the cross of current history. And the cross of current history throws shadows across all continents, even though Latin America is probably where the Mother of the Poor enters into the people's survival techniques most explicitly. How fortunate they are to have her.

To conclude, let us look through one last window onto the sufferings of poor women, imagining what they have to go through if they are to lead good lives, lives faithful to consciences that tell them they ought to procure the happiness of their families. Specifically, let us consider three paragraphs from a United Nations report on worldwide shifts in the status of women during the period 1970-90, keeping in mind Mary, the homeless mother, giving birth to her child as a migrant in a foreign land:

> Over the past two decades, women have increasingly moved to new homes in rural areas, urban areas and different countries, temporarily or permanently. Migrant women are vulnerable because they leave family and social networks and bring along few skills and resources. They also face physical hardships and dangers—as well as serious adjustment problems—because of their religion, language and nationality.
>
> Women migrants have greater economic opportunities in cities, but remain poor and are denied decent living conditions. In developing regions, over 70 per cent of the migrants to urban areas are under the age of 25 and 40 per cent are under 15. Girls under 15 make up the majority of female migrants in many Latin American countries, in some African countries, for example Ghana and Morocco, and Asian countries, for example Bangladesh, the Islamic Republic of Iran and Syria. In India only 4 per cent of the women migrate for employment reasons, 47 per cent because of marriage.
>
> Women who remain in rural areas but whose husbands migrate to urban areas find themselves with even more family and economic responsibilities. A few receive remittances, but most do not, making them widows in all but name. In Lesotho, where 45 per cent of rural households were headed by women in 1980, one survey found that fewer than half those women received any

money at all from their absent men. Research in Paki-
stan and India showed that migrant men sent remit-
tances to their fathers—to pay debts or buy land—rather
than to their wives.[11]

Christian feminist ethicists are bound to think that, on the
one hand, the situation of Latin American migrant women
shows how impotent the Christian tradition has often been.
On the other hand, the Christian tradition offers non-Christian traditions, such as those of India, reasons to rethink the
ties between women and men, wives and husbands, so that
women and children left behind by migrants might seem as
important as fathers and land.

A feminist sensitivity to questions of social justice is bound
to keep chanting, like a dirge, that women and children are
the leading victims of the poverty that dysfunctional, often
unjust social structures create worldwide. A Christian sensitivity is bound to keep chanting, like an antiphon, that the
poor are especially blessed by God, and thus that women and
children are the bulk of the citizenry of heaven. This does not
create a potent economic theory or ethics to replace the old,
impotent ones, but it does go to the roots of all viable ethical
programs, offering people the existential word they most long
to hear: No situation lies outside the pale of God's grace; no
situation is beyond redemption.

❧ 4 ❧

Sexual Morality

The "Impurity" of Women

We have considered issues of social justice, including black and Latin American dimensions of women's subjugation. In this chapter we consider the sexual abuses to which women the world over have been liable. Our first topic, the supposedly inherent impurity of women, comes to clarity in an essay by Indian Christian feminist Aruna Gnanadason. She begins with the ancient prejudices of India reflected in the *Ramayana*, one of India's most beloved epic myths:

> Sita, the great heroine of the *Ramayana*, is not accepted by her husband, Rama [the divine hero], who says, "Whatever I did was for the sake of avoiding scandal in every way, for clearing the name of the reputed dynasty. . . . You have been looked at by Ravana with his vicious eyes and have been molested on his lap. How can I accept you as such and sully my great family?" Sita then enters into the fire to prove to her husband her purity and adherence to the code of chastity.
>
> Based on this episode a contemporary Tamil novelist, Jayakantan, wrote a story entitled *Agni Pravesam* ("Entering the Fire") in 1966. A girl, in Jayakantan's story, while waiting for a bus on a rainy day, accepts a lift from a man who is driving by. He seduces her. She

narrates this incident with fear and tears to her mother on her return home. The mother at first is shocked, but after that she bathes her daughter in water, telling her that the water is the fire that will purify her. I add here a comment of the writer and literary critic C.S. Lakshmi: "Whether by water or fire, that the episode called for a process of purification itself was an evidence that the umbilical cord with tradition was not cut off."

In spite of the fact that Jayakantan could go that far and no further, as far as women's rights were concerned, the novel whipped up strong protests from writers and the public. Many of the voices of censure were, unfortunately, from women. They were enraged that the heroine was alive after the incident. Such characters are usually killed or are maimed in some way. It was considered an outrage against Tamil culture that Jayakantan had allowed the woman to go scot-free. Many counterstories were written almost as if in an attempt to blot out from the readers' minds the shameless episode. This is just one example to show how the myth of the inherent evil in women is sustained in the Indian psyche.[1]

What are the main overtones that Christian feminist ethicists ought to hear in this report? First, they ought to note the mythic voice. The imagery borrowed from the *Ramayana* is not accidental. Popular Indian morality continues to be shaped by the great epic poems that display ideal masculinity and femininity. The great myths teach both sexes how to think and feel about one another. The sad reality seems to be that the ancient prejudices against female nature are passed along to each new generation. Because the epics are the staff of traditional Indian culture, their sexist depictions of females, both divine and human, keep corrupting the Indian psyche age after age.

Inherent in Rama's reaction to Sita is both an irrational fear of female nature and an inordinate concern for sexual "purity." Rama cannot believe that Sita has been faithful to him during his long absences. In fact, she has been, but there is no way that she can prove her fidelity. On one level, the myth seems to glorify the fidelity of Sita and female human nature, suggesting that women are much purer than men. But on another, more decisive level, Rama stands for the divinely ideal male, so his suspicions of Sita amount to a sanction of men's fears that women are intrinsically corrupt. Just as the Israelite prophets did harm to countless generations of Jewish and Christian women by painting the sins of Israel as harlotry, so the mythopoets responsible for the great Hindu epics tilted traditional Indian culture against women.

Patriarchal cultures regularly are guilty of this sin. If the canonical works that they set at the center of their imaginations are biased against women, such cultures are bound to think that cynicism toward women, or even regular punishment of women, is right and proper. In the present case, the mythical background makes unacceptable a presentation of seduction that even slightly honors the greater responsibility of the male. The actual action of the story makes the girl quite innocent. But by thinking that the girl needs to be purified, her mother connives with the social prejudice that women have to be guilty—have to have "wanted it." Where the washing ought to be a cleansing of a filthy offense against the woman's entire being, the mother implies that the girl, like Sita, has to make recompense for the judgment of guilt sure to be passed against her, even though factually that judgment is wrong.

It does not matter that the girl has not actually done wrong. Simply because she is a woman, her culture considers her to be wanton. The deepest misfortune in this story is not what happened to the girl, degrading as that was. The deepest misfortune is the mother's initiation of the girl into accepting patriarchal Indian society's estimates of her female nature. The mother is saying, with the age-old tradition, that femaleness is wanton below the level of consent or refusal. The girl, as a typical female, has no substantial say in whether she is virtuous or loose. If an irregular sexual activity occurred, she must have been the cause. By placing her corrupt femininity in proximity to a masculinity naturally unable to restrain itself, she was responsible for the seduction and her consequent sullying.

The popular reaction to the story reinforces this interpretation. The majority of those outraged were not defenders of the girl's innocence but advocates of a much harsher punishment. They thought that not having her killed or maimed implied approbation of her conduct. Approbation was a horrible thought, because it introduced the novel, reckless notion that women might not be intrinsically corrupt. They might be moral or immoral exactly as men are, by the ordered or disordered exercise of their human freedom. This was so revolutionary a possibility that the majority of readers could not bear it. If they were to accept it, they might challenge the foundations of traditional Indian culture. Traditional Indian culture greatly curtailed the freedoms of women, largely because it thought women constantly needed the control of men. Without direction by first their fathers, then their husbands, and finally their eldest sons, women could never go through the life-cycle virtuously. It was part of female nature to be promiscuous, ever inclined to lust. Thus it was the natural obligation of men to control women and never to trust them.

It is not accidental that the man in the story gets off scot-free. He seduces the girl, but she is responsible for this wrongdoing, so he is not to blame. If a sin occurs between the sexes, the Indian prejudice is that the female is responsible. Women must live with the double-bind that, on the one hand, they are corrupt by nature, but on the other hand, they have to safeguard traditional morality. It is only a short step from this double-bind to the double license of men. Men can push onto women the responsibility for ethical relations between the sexes, and men can blame women for their lusts.

In fact, many Indians, both males and females, would not blame the man in the story for raping the girl—seducing her violently, completely against her will. Female nature is so corrupt that it is hard for men to sin against it. In raping women, men only give women what women want and deserve. Certainly this is a debased, wholly self-serving logic, but it functions in more countries than India. In fact, everywhere the root of much violence against women is a despising of female nature because it is considered constitutionally sensual, promiscuous, inclined to pull men from their lofty heights into the mire of sexual desire.

The Western equivalent to this deep-seated bias against women as constitutionally corrupt appears in the biblical and post-biblical treatments of Eve, the first woman.[2] The popular Christian view was that Eve had begun the process by which humanity fell into its sorry state. Had Eve not listened to the serpent and eaten the fruit, human nature would have remained incorrupt. Had Eve not held such sway over Adam, he might have resisted the process and saved humankind. But Eve in effect seduced Adam. He was no match for her blandishments. So, in the opinion of many of the Church fathers, the daughters of Eve always bear close watching. The lusts of men are so powerful that women represent a grave danger to men's salvation.

Not accidentally, many of the fathers extolled the celibate life as more virtuous than the married life. Men wanting to become holy, to please God, would do themselves a great favor by separating from women completely. Equally, women wanting to be virtuous ought to become consecrated virgins. The friction between the sexes is such that anyone serious about holiness would try to bypass it. Granted, this took the Church fathers some distance from Genesis itself, where sexual love is not disparaged. On the other hand, even in Genesis we find prominent the tendency of the man to blame the woman when things common to both go wrong. Genesis may be lampooning Adam when it shows him trying to pass the blame for the primal disobedience onto Eve, but the story itself plants the seed of suspicion. Perhaps men do have to make certain they stay free of women's overtures. Perhaps men's loss of rule is at the root of human disorders. Many readers of Genesis have thought this way. Patriarchal Judaism and Christianity owe big debts to this way of thinking.

In passing, I note that the depreciation of female nature that we find in patriarchal cultures explains much in the widespread practice of letting female infants die. Even today, parents in India, China, and many other countries are far more

likely to abandon little girls than little boys. The advent of
new techniques for determining the sex of the fetus has only
given such misogynism new scope. How many abortions arise
from the parents' rejecting the prospect of having a girl is
uncertain, but many physicians and counselors report suspicions that fetuses are being aborted for being of the wrong
sex. Almost always the cases involve females. Rarely do parents want a girl so strongly that they abort a boy.

In traditional societies males head the families, make the
prayers and sacrifices that ensure the peace of the ancestors,
and ensure the parents against the perils of old age. Females
leave the family when they marry, entering the extended
household of their husbands. Females bring their parents little economic benefit. Indeed, even to marry females off is
expensive, since the parents must provide a dowry. The irony
in India is that even with a dowry, even having found a new
home, women are not safe. Suspiciously large numbers of
daughters-in-law commit suicide early in their marriages. The
probability is that most of them are actually murdered. The
groom and his family have received the bride's dowry, so,
unless she proves exceptionally pleasing, they have little reason to expect much further benefit from her.

Even when the woman in fact is not murdered but freely
commits suicide, the most frequent reason is that she has suffered physical or emotional abuse in her new home and so
become miserably unhappy. In the eyes of many Indians,
though, women's miseries are insignificant, because female
nature is insignificant. Just as Sita was far less important than
Rama, so any Indian woman can be dismissed as relatively
unimportant compared to her male counterpart.

On the necessary Christian feminist ethical response to this
state of affairs we can be brief. Any denigration of female
nature is unacceptable. Any treatment of women that is not
evenhanded must be rejected. Women have all the dignity of
men. Women have been redeemed by the blood of Christ just
as men have. No patriarchal structures, whether outside
Christianity or inside, can take priority over these bedrock
truths. Even if the Christian Churches themselves denigrate

female nature or do not treat women evenhandedly, Christian feminist ethicists have to stand firm.

The entire edifice of faith crumbles if one half of humanity is lesser than the other. Were that to happen, God the Creator could not be trusted, and God the Redeemer would fail. Thus, one's estimate of female nature is no small, accidental matter. It goes to the heart of one's goodness as a human being, one's authenticity as a Christian. If female human nature is tainted as male human nature is not, human existence is morally absurd.

The Body of Women

One of the interesting, significant characteristics of much feminist religious reflection is a desire for a healthy embodiment that will offset the unhealthy dualisms of patriarchal thinking. In a recent essay on the redemption of the body, with special reference to Christian patriarchal traditions, Paula M. Cooey makes several effective points.

First, drawing on the prison writings of the Argentinean exile Alicia Partnoy, Cooey reminds us that in many countries jail cells teem with people being bodily abused. Partnoy's crime was participation in the Peronista Youth Movement. For such participation, she and her husband were carted off with no concern for their nine-month-old daughter. Their routine in prison ran as follows:

> Lunch was at 1:00 P.M.; we went without food for eighteen consecutive hours daily. We were constantly hungry. I lost 20 pounds, going down to 95 pounds (I am 5 ft. 5 in.). Added to the meager food, the lack of sugar or fruits, was the constant state of stress that made our bodies consume calories rapidly. We ate our meals blindfolded, sitting on the bed, plate in lap. When we had soup or watery stew, the blows were constant because the guards insisted that we keep our plates straight. When we were thirsty, we asked for water, receiving only threats or blows in response. For talking

we were punished with blows from a billy jack, punches, or removal of our mattresses. The atmosphere of violence was constant. The guards put guns to our heads or mouths and pretended to pull the trigger.[3]

This is a miniature of all the violence visited on the human body throughout patriarchal history. It reminded Partnoy, and she reminds us, of the centrality of bread, and all the other basic bodily needs. The eucharistic symbolism became deeper, but also more accusing: Partnoy could only condemn the clergy (the celebrants of the eucharist) who cooperated with military rulers who would degrade people's bodies in these ways. Cooey forges creative links to the other forms of bodily oppression that women, especially, have suffered:

The ethical dimensions of the redemption of the body are gynocentric, or woman-centered. Unless a specifically female human face appears as necessarily characteristic of the oppressed with whom we seek solidarity in protest, then Christians have misunderstood the full depth of the oppression that requires redress; the redemption of the body, whether the human body or the planet Earth, cannot be made real. In the first place, the human oppressed, regardless of age, class, race, ethnicity, or creed, are peopled predominantly by women against whom violence is directed specifically because they are female human beings. From abortion, infanticide, and neglect of females because they are not sons, to dowry death, genital mutilation, forced pregnancy, and beating of adult women, viewed as property of their actual or potential husbands, violence against women comprises at present the greatest violation of human rights throughout the earth. In the second place, by virtue of the symbolic identification and devaluation of "woman" with "nature," correlative with the symbolic identification and elevation of "man" with "spirit," this violence extends to environmental abuse and annihilation as well.[4]

So, the body is a central ethical, feminist, and Christian concern. When people mistreat human bodies, whether those of others or their own, they mistreat human selves. We don't have human selves apart from bodies. For the mundane tasks of an earthly ethics, we have to deal with people who have skin on, can bleed, are full of feelings. Our bodies are always sexed, and our sex shapes us through and through. If any culture despises one sex, or exalts one sex at the expense of the other, it denies the realities of human embodiment.

Paradoxically enough, this often occurs most gruesomely when cultures lack transcendence. Having no significant outreach to God, they cannot see the body as sacramental. It shrinks to mere animality or mechanism. So people can abuse the body as they wish: with drugs, violence, aberrant sex, slave labor. I think Cooey passes by the abuses inflicted on male bodies throughout history, which give the sexes some equality in bearing physical degradation, but I agree that women have been the more abused sex. For the patriarchal mavens of cultural power, the female body has been both dirtier than the male and purer. The result has been to make the female body less real, and so more easily manipulated, abused, disregarded. The irony, of course, is that all bodily life begins in women. One need only look at the phenomenon of abortion, though, to see how many perverse forces fight might and main to deny this God-given beginning.

The major slips that Cooey makes occur when she tries to redo the Christian theological tradition, in order to fix what has become broken in our views of the human body. The heart of the problem, as she sees it, is a reading of the data about Jesus that, by making him divine, takes away his real humanity. As I see it, Cooey makes a valiant effort to reinterpret the significance of Jesus' humanity but a hash of the traditional teaching about his full reality. By opposing his two natures, and asking that the hypostatic union (their connection) be something patent to her own intelligence, she vitiates the mystery that attends all of God's doings, especially those of the Incarnate Logos. In the name of the Old Testament prohibition on graven images, she gives what is finally a Jew-

ish or Muslim reading of the Incarnation, according to which
Jesus cannot be God.

Cooey does not think this takes away salvation. Indeed, she
thinks it makes salvation more effective. Much in her desire
for a better contemporary Christological language is admirable, but inasmuch as she lacks a firm commitment to specifically Christian faith (the creedal assertion that the Word
that became flesh was God from God, Light from Light, true
God from true God), she ends up with a reduced Jesus and
so a diminished Christology.

Consider, for example, the following paragraph:

> In other words, an alternative view of the incarnation,
> one perhaps more attuned to both biblical and twenti-
> eth-century sensibilities, claims that Jesus saves us by
> directing our attention through the events of his life,
> death, and resurrection as narrated in scripture, to God
> at work throughout creation, upholding nature and act-
> ing through human activity in history, to restore and
> reconcile all life, including life usually considered the
> least noteworthy. Interpreted in this manner incarna-
> tion is always going on, but Jesus in relation to others
> remains pivotal as the specific revelatory source by
> which those who call their faith Christian come to rec-
> ognize, and by grace, quite literally to re-member divine
> activity at work throughout nature and history. Jesus
> thus retains epistemological and soteriological centrality
> for Christian faith without reference to his ontological
> status, in this respect relieving him of the burden of
> idolatry [5]

I find it a novel idea for Christians that faith in the divinity
of Jesus should be idolatrous. Similarly, I find it impossible
to retain the epistemological and soteriological centrality of
Jesus without reference to his ontological status. From the
Johannine theology of the New Testament (whose grant of
priority to Word over flesh in the Prologue Cooey rejects),
through the creeds and conciliar documents, and continuing
through the history of Christian spirituality (consider, for

example, Julian of Norwich's exegesis of the bodily sufferings of Christ), the steady chorus has been that Jesus is *both* fully divine *and* fully human. Break this unity and you dissolve the bond of Christianity; you fracture the bones of Christ's Body. For what benefit? To have a savior like us in all things including sin? To deny that once and for all God assumed our estate and spoke the yes of reconciliation into our marrow? To conciliate Jews, Muslims, Buddhists, and others for whom the Incarnation is a scandal? To reform the faith for which so many martyrs died?

In most of my inner debates with Church officials,[6] I find myself advocating more accommodation to the signs of the times, the breathings of the Holy Spirit. Here, however, I feel brought to a line drawn in the sand. Cross from traditional Christological orthodoxy into Cooey's territory and you have abandoned the faith long handed down, a faith that has survived more radical challenges than those now posed by feminist ethicists. Ironically, many prior challenges were more radical precisely because they were ontological directly, and not merely by implication. Arius, for example, said there was a then when the Logos was not. Inference: the Logos came into being, was made rather than eternally generated. (Cooey finds such distinctions as generated/made nugatory.) Arius' conclusion: the Word was not strictly divine, was in an ultimate sense created. Further heterodox conclusions: there was no radical salvation, and so both the Christian scriptures and the Christian liturgy have been lying.

The extent of one's commitment to the traditional ontological status accorded Jesus as divine depends on one's appreciation of what the original Christians saw, what the great cloud of subsequent witnesses has experienced. If this vision, this experience, is dispensable, then of course it makes no difference whether Jesus is more than a functional savior — more than the one God used to work exemplary deeds. But if this vision, this experience, is the pith of human healing from the literally deadly diseases of the created spirit, angelic as well as human, then Jesus has to be God from God, Light from Light.

Nothing but God can make us from nothingness, redeem

us from the nothingness of evil, innoculate us with eternity so that our morality does not do us in. For traditional Christian faith we become deathless, because we become partakers of the deathless divine nature. We do not do this in or of ourselves. We do this in God, more precisely in God's Word become flesh, who centers the universal economy of salvation.

Of course we can't understand such claims literally, denotatively, apart from the living tutelage of the Spirit of Christ, who is God's love without beginning or end. Of course only the great saints, the mystics dramatically transformed into Christ in their lifetime, get more than the barest inkling. But to call this traditional sense of the human vocation, based on this traditional understanding of the divinity and humanity of Jesus, no longer relevant to contemporary men and women is to condemn contemporary men and women to much less significance than their forebears enjoyed.

Their forebears knew, in the conviction of faith, that the ground of their being, the end of their time, was an embrace by God, sacramentalized by what had happened in Jesus, that fulfilled their humanity, body and spirit, by taking it into divinity. They knew that earth would finally be fair and all her people wise, because of the eschatological Christ, whose ontological status was divine. I would never castigate at great length anyone trying to minister to the religious illiteracy of contemporary Christians, let alone pagans. That's a marvelous work, and one only for the valiant. But I have to wonder, gently, how such ministry will ever come about, if the ministers don't care about the bedrock foundations of their tradition, in this case their Christian tradition.

There is no historically recognizable, authentic, orthodox Christianity without a mainframe confession of the full divinity of Jesus, as there is none without an equally central confession of his full humanity. Traditional Christology is as bald as that. Certainly this orthodoxy has been abused, interpreted narrowly and meanly, used as a club. Certainly such abuse continues to be the temptation, perhaps even the actual sin, of some Church leaders today, especially in my Roman Catholic communion. But, I believe, the high Christological tradition itself is beautiful and true beyond compare. Nothing matches it in the history of religions, and no reach of contemporary feminist ethicists that I have seen even comes up to its knee.

Child Abuse

The disservice done to Christ by some contemporary feminist theologies is further illustrated by Rita Nakashima Brock's efforts to correlate classical trinitarian theology with child abuse:

> Classical trinitarian formulas confuse parent and child and husband and wife, such that the father and son, or husband and wife, become one person and such that the father is seen to live some aspect of his own life in his son. Such confusion reflects male-dominant values in which all subordinates to the reigning patriarch are considered extensions of his identity. The confusion, which leads to fusion, is then repeated in the hierarchical bride-groom images of Christ and Church. The circularity, abstractness, and incoherence of trinitarian doctrines indicate to me that they tend to reinforce a sense of fusion, which is part of human experience, but which cannot satisfy finally our deepest spiritual needs for images of intimacy. Real intimacy can be grounded only in the contextual, unique, and particular, and in self-awareness. And intimacy is virtually impossible in systems of dominance and abuse.
>
> As an aspect of trinitarian thought, Christology is often based in implicit elements of child abuse. Jesus, in his human aspect, is sacrificed as the one perfect child. His sacrifice upholds the righteousness of the father who otherwise would require obedience from his incapable, sinful children. We are, it is asserted, born with a tragic flaw, and therefore must depend upon the perfect father and other persons with authority to reveal the truth. The punishment earned by us all is inflicted on the one perfect child. Then the father can forgive his wayward

creation and love it. The doctrinal dependence upon patriarchal gender systems becomes clear when god as mother is substituted for father. The doctrines are not only virtually incomprehensible, the very suggestion of such substitutions raises enormous negative emotional reactions.[7]

What is wrong with this approach? A great deal. First, it comes from outside Christian faith. It is not a theological statement, an effort to understand what one has accepted as the crux of one's life, the essence of one's salvation. Certainly the crux of one's life and the essence of one's salvation have historical dimensions. Certainly, as they actually work themselves out, they entail specific cultural assumptions, associations, and limitations. But, for what I would call orthodox, healthy Christian faith, God enjoys a carte blanche, based on the astounding good news of the deeds of God in Christ. One makes sense of traditional trinitarian language only by reading the New Testament and the Church fathers after having accepted this good news, granted this carte blanche. To attempt to fit traditional faith to new patterns completely at variance with them is to assure incomprehension and distortion. In a nutshell, it is bad theological method.

Second, when we grant that the traditional trinitarian symbols are precious but faltering analogies for explicating the reality and teaching of Jesus, as the New Testament hands those on, we are not confused by the relations reported between the Father and the Son. Jesus calls the divinity familiar to the Jews of his day "Father." Might he, in other circumstances, have added that this divinity could also be called "Mother"? Certainly. May we, today, emphasize that feminine attributes apply to God as well, and as poorly, as masculine? Certainly. But the first proper move is to understand the language attributed to Jesus on its own terms, which neither necessitate child abuse nor sanction it. Moreover, the language attributed to Jesus is not obscure. He says that God deals with him like a loving Father, in whom he can trust completely. He comports himself toward the Father like a loving Son. In light of the resurrection of Jesus and the send-

ing of the Holy Spirit, early Christian speculation made the
relation between Father and Son constitutive of divinity itself.
It did the same for the relations among Father, Son, and
Spirit. All of this was faltering analogy, and yet it was finally
judged better than any other language that the early Christians had managed to fashion.

Nowadays we note the lack of feminine imagery in the original Christian language about God. (In fact, such imagery
occurs from time to time in both Testaments. The Holy Spirit,
for instance, often seems to move like a brooding, mothering
divinity. The motif that Jesus represents the Wisdom of God,
a feminine figure in Jewish thought of Jesus' day, breaks any
macho stranglehold on the interpretation of Jesus' divinity or
humanity.) Thus we realize that there is room for further
theological speculation, as long (I would say) as one keeps
faith with the original revelation couched in Jesus' language
about the Father, Son, and Spirit.

Clearly no doctrine is ethical if it leads directly to the abuse
of children, women, slaves, Jews, or any other portion of the
human family. But what in the traditional trinitarian imagery
does this? To claim that the patriarchal overtones of a divine
Father punishing a representative Son render this imagery
immoral is to reach much farther than I find legitimate. The
doctrines of satisfaction that developed in the history of Christian theology have their limitations, but they could never blot
out the manifest stress of the New Testament on God's love
nor establish ethical codes justifying the abuse of children or
any other human beings. If anything, such doctrines sought
to establish the extremity of Jesus' freely chosen love for his
Father and his fellow human beings. Can any reputable Christian, any person who has experienced something of the divine
love, gainsay the goodness of this love?

The far better application of Christian imagery to the problem of child abuse comes from contemplation of the Christ-
child. In both the New Testament and the mainstream of
Christian art, the nativity of Christ is a sign of God's ineffable
condescension to humankind. In being born of Mary, the Son
of God found a way to step out of divinity and join it to
humanity. The tender intimacy between Madonna and child

is but a pale figure of the intimacy that God established in the Virgin's womb, when something literally beyond our understanding occurred. Divinity became the inmost identity of humanity. The eternal reality of the Word became the inmost "Who" of Jesus, his ontological basis. This destroyed none of the human psychology of Jesus. In fact, it perfected his human psychology, for the rule in dealings between creatures and their Creator is that intimacy with the Creator increases the distinctive identities of creatures. We become ourselves in the measure we say yes to God, surrender ourselves into God's keeping, not in the measure we try to stand apart, in prideful autonomy.

It does not matter whether the imagery through which we surrender ourselves into God's keeping makes God paternal or maternal. What matters is that God be open-armed, warmhearted. Surely that is the meaning of the parable of the Prodigal Son and the parable of the woman who sweeps her house to find her lost coin? And surely that takes the Christian God to the utter extremes from any sanctioning of child abuse. It is admirable for people like Brock to want to picture God afresh, perhaps as a maternal figure, and to speculate about the changes in Christian spirituality that such a picture entails. But they ought to know what they are doing when they fashion new images for God, just as they ought to know what they are doing when they deal with traditional trinitarian images.

We should remember that God is always more unlike what we say than like it. We have only frail analogies. Unless we let ourselves be persuaded by the utter goodness of God, we make huge mistakes in our theology. Unless we open ourselves to the full depth and breadth of the Christian tradition, we repeat wrong steps taken centuries ago apparently blissfully unaware. The basic intent of the traditional Christian view of God is not patriarchal. It establishes no dominion of men over women, no bullying of either sex by a heavenly overlord. The basic intent of the traditional Christian view of God is to proclaim a love so complete it has opened both the heavens and the earth for human beings' delight.

Yes, there are strands of Scripture, and more than strands

of Christian historical performance, that are regrettably patriarchal. And, yes, one has to pick the wheat from the chaff, which demands becoming judicious, taught by the Spirit of God. But this process does not require establishing one's own canon of Scripture. Rather, it ought to require listening to all the voices of Scripture with a keen ear for Christ's voice and a clear memory of the centrality he gave to love.

When we manage such an interpretational stance, we move beyond annoyance at tendentious attacks on the Trinity, such as Brock's, simply regretting that so little has been rightly understood and so much mystagogy has been lost. By such a move beyond, what was clear at the outset, but slipped away in a blur of horror at the maiming of orthodox Christian faith, can return to focus. Of course one has to sympathize with all those hurt by the abuse of children. Of course one has to correct misinterpretations of scriptural passages and traditional teachings that have developed through the centuries. I myself have spent considerable time in women's shelters trying to explain why "spare the rod" cannot mean breaking the faces of women or children. Many other women, and men, have done a great deal more.

All this is necessary and good work. But it will not be accomplished by the substitution of a feminist divinity manufactured in reaction against, not the proper use of trinitarian or Christological images and teachings, but bastardized forms not known to be illegitimate. It will not be accomplished in Christian terms unless people face the mysteriousness of all our dealings with God, and all our truly profound human needs, and let the vision that Jesus disclosed be the guiding wisdom. Anything else is little more than straw, as Thomas Aquinas found toward the end of a life spent in a heroic effort to understand his faith.

Present-day Christian feminists will also find their many words to be straw, less mystically and more culpably, if they do not focus them on Christ, God's power and wisdom. If God is as Jesus showed God to be, the Trinity is the source and pattern of what makes us most human: our knowing and our loving. If God is as Jesus showed God to be, the most

abused child is the one led away from the love of God the
Father or God the Mother.

A Lesbian Feminist Voice on Christ

As I have examined my reaction to feminist attacks on traditional Christology and trinitarian theory, I have noted an
increasingly clear distinction between what is central to Christian faith and what is peripheral. The traditional saying, "In
necessary things, unity; in doubtful things, liberty; in all
things, charity," has begun to sing in my blood. With Karl
Rahner, I believe that the cardinal mysteries of Christian faith
are the Trinity, the Incarnation, and grace. About these there
must be unity—adherence to the full spirit, if not the exact
letter, of "what has been believed always, everywhere, and by
all"—Vincent of Lerins' description of catholicity.

No doubt there are other articles of the Christian creed
that are necessary for catholic faith, including articles about
the centrality of the Church (though hardly about the specific
forms of its government). Still, I find few determinations of
Christians' lifestyles. Beyond the general injunctions to love
neighbor as self and keep the ten commandments, most of
Christian moral behavior seems a matter of discerning the
spirits, learning the ways of Christian prudence.

Admittedly, the traditional glosses on the ten commandments tended to swell them into comprehensive legal entities.
Like the rabbis who kept expanding the Torah, the Christian
moralists and canonists keep expanding their received codes.
The rabbis had a more ingenious rationale: the fuller the law,
the less chance of offending God by inadvertence and the
more chance of pleasing God by observance. The Christian
moralists seldom bothered to make their decrees palatable.
Perhaps the example of Jesus in his battles with the Pharisees
hung over their shoulder, making it hard in good conscience
to lay more burdens on the faith of Jesus' simple followers.
Listening to Jesus, it was hard to fend off the voice saying,
"The sabbath was made for human beings, not human beings
for the sabbath—or the financial support of the Church, or

the fulfillment of local mores." Thus, the Christian canonists often paid little attention to Jesus.

All this is by way of explaining why I distinguish so sharply between what I take to be mistakes in cardinal faith and legitimate options in Christian lifestyle, including sexual orientation. To bridge the way to a legitimation of one "deviant" lifestyle, that of a loving lesbianism, let me draw on the crisp, elegant, moving Christology of Carter Heyward:

> The focus, albeit controversial, in modern Anglicanism on the incarnational character of the whole creation testifies to how seriously Anglicans may take the profoundly sacramental constitution of our world. Nowhere is this significant emphasis any more apparent than in the contemporary efforts of feminist liberation theologians to offer images of incarnation that do justice to the whole earth and its inhabitants, not merely to the christological preserves of Church fathers.
>
> The whole inhabited earth is sacred space in which God lives, breathes, and acts. Sharing this common home, we are One Body. Insofar as we live as such, we reflect the trinitarian character of God as the Lover, the Beloved, and the spirit of Love which hands the Lover to her Beloved. As people created for the purpose of loving one another, all of us are worthy of love—and are responsible for loving. This worthiness and this responsibility, ours by birth, constitutes our holiness and requires that we live in common-wealth, so that all persons and other creatures can live together creatively.
>
> Richard Hooker, a preeminent father of Anglicanism, understood our sacramental heritage as rooted in our "participation" with Christ—"he in us and us in him"—through the liturgy as well as through our general corporate life as the Church. The "participation" that Hooker commended provides a useful means of envisioning our moral life and our work together in solidarity with the poor, women, elderly citizens, gay men and lesbians, members of racial, ethnic, and religious minorities, and all marginalized people. From a feminist

liberation perspective, we are able to understand our relationship to Jesus as one of participation. We are *with* Jesus; as such we are *in* Christ.[8]

There is much more that one could say on each of these points, some of which Heyward herself has said in other places. My delight here lies with her careful effort to speak in chorus with Christian tradition, even as she notes new directions in which that tradition must go. The incarnational character of the whole creation can be rooted in such biblical texts as the Prologue of John's gospel and the first chapter of Colossians. They stimulated the patristic figures and scholastics who pondered what creation in the divine Word-to-be-made-flesh has entailed.

Such an incarnationalism also reflects our current twentieth-century awareness that no matter is foreign to God — opposed to divinity, as prior dichotomies between matter and spirit assumed. God is more unlike our understanding of "spirit" than like it. God can be closer to matter, more ingredient in matter, than we can imagine. Thus any creature, seen against the backdrop of the creative power holding it in being and so sensed to be a presence of God, can be sacramental.

The history of the world's religions is in many ways a history of sacramental theophanies. Streams and mountains, storms and quiet times, bears and eagles have all brought God to mind. Therefore the feminist liberation theologians who want to deepen our appreciation of the divine presence in creation and show how it grounds the value of many creatures we tend to consider valueless move from a sure religious, Christological instinct. If the earth is God's and the fullness thereof, then all God's creatures have something holy at their cores, something entitling them to kindly, appreciative treatment. An ecological revolution lurks in these simple theses, as does a restoration to dignity of many people cast to the margins by prior history, most of which has been patriarchal.

I am not sure what images of incarnation Heyward has in mind when she seeks to do justice to the whole earth and its inhabitants or what Christological preserves of Church fathers she wishes to break open. My own position is that

images of incarnation work best when they radiate from the
Incarnate Word, taken as the prime instance of divine
enfleshment. I also hold that the most faithful interpretation
of the Incarnate Word both does not divorce him from the
historical Jesus, de facto a male, and does not make him a
prop of patriarchy (the depreciation of females).

That the whole inhabited earth is sacred space in which
God lives, breathes, and acts is a glorious conflation of biblical
conviction and traditional Christian metaphysics. We human
beings make one body, with our fellow non-human creatures
as well as with our human brothers and sisters. The tacit link
in Heyward's inference that when we live out this truth we
reflect the trinitarian character of our God, who is love, is that
our bond with other creatures is love—we make one body
because we are bonded in affection, want to live in union. To
describe the trinitarian God as the "Lover, the Beloved, and
the spirit of Love" seems to me a legitimate variation on quite
traditional understandings of the three persons.

God insofar as traditionally called Father is in all ways the
source, the underived origin of the godhead and creation
alike. To call God the Lover underscores why God both is by
nature and freely chooses to be diffusive of the divine goodness. God insofar as traditionally called Son is the Beloved of
the Father (the Lover, the unoriginated source). The second
person is also the self-understanding of the Father, the movement of light from light through which the never-ending,
coruscant knowing of the first person is expressed. God insofar as traditionally called Spirit is the love uniting first and
second persons, Father and Son, Lover and Beloved.

Whether one follows the Eastern Orthodox view that the
Spirit proceeds from the Father through the Son, or the Western view that the Spirit proceeds from the united action, the
mutually spirative love, of the first two persons seems to me
irrelevant at this juncture. We may interpret Heyward's "she"
for God as having assimilated trinitarian love to a primacy of
the feminine, and so having opened the possibility that lesbian
love moves in its reflection. This seems to me fine. Again and
again all honest theologians state that their analogies are
more unlike than like divinity itself. Whatever does not offend

against the innermost notions, which in the case of the Trinity are (a) three fully equal, only relationally distinct, "persons" (unlimited centers of consciousness) and (b) one identical divine essence, is legitimate. Of course, the correlation of these notions is a mystery, boggling the mind. But by holding to the innermost notions one can fend off offenses against the mystery, including those from rationalists, whether feminists such as Cooey and Brock or not, who want to cut the Trinity down to what they can understand. I do not find these innermost notions determined to masculine sexual imagery, so I find no difficulty in Heyward's playing with a new set of figures. The final nexus of the paragraph is a tacit argument that, having been made in the image and likeness of a God of love, we are both held to loving and constituted worthy of love.

Hooker's notion of participation offers a good way to think about the body that we form in Christ. The life of the Trinity that we receive in and through Christ makes sharing as primary as being independent. God is three persons as fundamentally as one nature. In the liturgy, through our faith, and in our works of solidarity, we activate the participatory structure of our Christological being. When we stand alongside people in need, people suffering on the margins, we edge into their lives. When we take them to heart, make their needs our intentions, we enter into the heart of Christ, the life of the vine animating all the branches.

I am gratified that Heyward uses the name Jesus for the one in whom we find our participatory being, vocation, and fulfillment. She permits no divorce between Jesus and Christ (though she does leave open the possibility of denotations of Christ that escape the historical limitations of the man Jesus). That seems to me crucial for orthodox Christian faith. I find no salvation in a Christology ashamed of the actual way that the grace of God worked in the eschatological action that pivoted on Jesus of Nazareth.

It remains to be seen what some Christian feminist ethicists might make of this participatory Christology for specific matters of social or sexual justice. On the whole, though, I am confident that one can work out the major goals of the different liberation theologies—feminist, gay, lesbian, ethnic, racial, ecological—as valid applications of the gospel, even imperatives of the gospel, as long as one derives any specifically Christian claims from participation in the definitive status of Jesus.

So, for example, to argue that same-sex love full of faith, self-sacrifice, commitment, and all the other things that one would ask of heterosexual love, is compatible with a participatory Christology seems to me fully legitimate. So does the argument that Christians ought to seek an active solidarity with all suffering peoples, regardless of their color, faith, or sexual orientation. Several further steps would have to become explicit on the way to elucidating such a liberational ethics based on a participatory Christology, but I suspect one could do this with little difficulty. The exemplary character of Jesus' life and love, along with the outreach implied in his divinity, supplies most of what one would need.

Marriage

In a volume commemorating one hundred years of Catholic social thought (the centennial of Pope Leo XIII's *Rerum Novarum*), Lisa Sowle Cahill has reflected on marriage as follows:

Perhaps the major challenge for a modern Western perspective on marriage is to set our assumptions about personal relations in marriage against a historical and cross-cultural horizon. Looked at more universally, both the importance of parenthood as a meaning of sexuality and socio-cultural linkage as a meaning of marriage and family have a prominence we Westerners are less inclined to notice than the importance of personal commitments and fulfillments. As Margaret Farley has observed, the marital commitment is a commitment to a whole framework of life, which sustains the love of the partners, but which also must be construed in terms of family, community, Church, and wider society. Catholic teaching needs to find a way to affirm the dignity, freedom, and happiness of persons in marriage and family while simultaneously linking parenthood, kinship, and social roles *to the integrity* of sex and marriage as intersubjective experiences that are also always embodied and social experiences. In other words, it is not enough to refer in sexual morality or marriage merely to the integrity of physical reproduction as such, or to tie the physical to the intersubjective in a forced or artificial way that does not ring true to the experience of married persons and parents. Spousehood and parenthood must be linked together as ongoing personal and embodied *relationships* that have a definitive sexual/procreative dimension, not through an analysis of *acts* of sexual intercourse.[9]

Let us examine this rich paragraph. Characteristic of modern Western assumptions about marriage is that the fulfillment of the partners stands at the forefront of the enterprise. If one compares this assumption with the prevailing attitudes about marriage that dominated past history in the West, or that continue to dominate many non-Western cultures today, one finds that the assumption is not something we should take for granted or consider obvious.

In other historical eras parenthood (procreating and rearing children) has been at least as important as personal fulfillment, and in many non-Western cultural areas it continues to be so today. Similarly, the social and economic ties that marriage creates have been as important as the desires of the individual spouses. Throughout history, most marriages have been arranged by the parents of the spouses, for reasons more complicated than simply the happiness of the young woman and man. For instance, prospective political and economic ties between the families have often weighed heavily.

We cannot separate the couple from the institutions into which their marriage takes them in new ways. They become fuller members of their neighborhoods, Churches, school districts, lives of their in-laws, and much more. The strength of so-called objective, unromantic views of marriage is that they tend to give the many social dimensions of marriage and family life their due. (The weakness of objective views can be their neglect of the romantic spark, the wonder, that makes the couple want to marry in the first place.)

Catholic social teaching, traditionally long on the objective appreciation of marriage, needs to strengthen its support of the spouses' personal fulfillment without losing its objective wisdoms. Pope John Paul II's desire to apply personalist philosophy to marriage has met some of this need, but much remains to be done. The ties between the couple's experience of sexual sharing and its integration into the larger worlds of parenting and community remain less clear than they could be. The ideal would be deeper theological appreciations of how intersubjective experiences such as sexual love always remain embodied, historical, connected to other people, current events, social trends, economic forces, and the like.

Cahill opposes her sophisticated, many-layered analysis of marriage and family life to an ethics of marital life that places the integrity of physical reproduction (birth control) at the center of the moral evaluation. The only adequate ethical view of marriage is one that does justice to the full span of experiences, issues, and needs involved. Individual acts of sexual intercourse lose much of their meaning, unless we place them in the context of the entire marital enterprise, especially the line of growth that it is following. One might also add, as Cahill does in other sections of her essay, the relevance of more biblical views of marriage, to the end of removing ethical questions from a juridical framework and placing them in the horizon of Christian discipleship—following Christ and responding to God's love.

Cahill rejects any idealized or stereotypical view of the roles of the two sexes in marriage. She opposes an archetypal sense of masculinity or femininity, favoring instead respect for the concrete individuality of the spouses involved. But there is nothing in her study that proclaims the demise of marriage in a feminist age.

I admire this option for sophistication rather than simplicism, and for hope rather than despair. However twisted by patriarchal views, the biblical sense that marital love is a symbol of the covenant of the God who has chosen to live with us human beings continues to reveal volumes about human fulfillment. If the divine has chosen to share our lives, for better or worse, for richer or poorer, then our lives are astoundingly meaningful. The immediate ethical inference should be that God partakes in whatever we do. There is no complete disjunction between "mine" and "thine." With God, as with a generous spouse, the operative word is *our*. Emboldened by this faith, Christian spouses can open their most trying difficulties to God. Questions of family planning, work, managing family resources, religious education, and anything else fall inside the covenant. God is not a patriarchal opponent of women's fulfillment, any more than of men's. The things spouses do to ensure a good family life are the things God is primed to support.

Presently we are a long way from either the view of God or the view of society at large implied in Cahill's prescriptions. Spouses will only feel invited to share their most intimate fears with God if God is not a canon lawyer, holding them to a code so objective it takes no coloring from their individual circumstances. Setting their moral choices about the size of their family, the distribution of their financial resources, and the application of their talents to social problems in the horizon of the larger society to which their marriage has connected them will only seem possible for Christian spouses if today's individualism and isolation cede to more communitarian orientations. Specifically, we will only have a fully appropriate marital ethics when we take into account the entire network of influences actually shaping people's marriages. Much more molds spouses than their own one-to-one attraction and love, however passionate. Moralists will only understand marital love fully when the entire tissue of relationships influenced by a marriage comes up for review.

This plea for greater awareness of context, relationships, social influences, and the like seems to me characteristically feminine. As such, it offers much to the traditionally blinkered, overly individualistic and abstract teachings on marital ethics that I associate with patriarchal ethics in general and Roman Catholic moral theology in particular. Admittedly,

things have changed for the better since Vatican Council II
(1962-65). Still, more remains to be done. I believe, for
instance, that moralists would be wise to join forces with ascet-
ical and mystical theologians to clarify the processes through
which people's consciousnesses become converted, enlight-
ened, sanctified. I believe better case studies of how good
people balance the many different claims made on their
resources and loyalties could be extremely helpful. My observation says that women often have a better sense than men
of the complexity of marital issues, perhaps especially those
involving children. Relatedly, women are often better attuned
to the emotional flow of the household and more convinced
that much work remains as long as the feelings of any family
member are hurting. These are further reasons for inviting
women to share more deeply in the enterprise of constructing
a new Christian marital ethics.

On the question of divorce, Cahill is again sophisticated:

> Indissolubility and sacramentality are ideas having nor-
> mative force but not inevitability. Sacramentality is never
> something which exists in a marriage wholly and com-
> pletely. Like commitment, fidelity, sexual consumma-
> tion, and parenthood, it is cumulative and progressive,
> taking root slowly, requiring nurturance to bear fruit.
> Although the presence of God to humans within the
> creaturely relationship is God's own gift, and, from the
> divine side, irrevocable, God accepts a certain vulnera-
> bility in choosing a human vehicle for self-disclosure.
> The marriage as a human relationship is a living,
> organic, and creaturely reality, never immune to death
> through neglect, destruction, or catastrophe. Marital
> disintegration must be recognized institutionally and
> redeemed practically through forgiveness, reconcilia-
> tion, and reparation—in the termination of the first
> spousal relation; in fidelity to its continuing claims, espe-
> cially those of children; and in building new relation-
> ships, for which more successful Christian transfor-
> mation can be hoped.[10]

Divorce is a case in which the messy character of most human achievements and failures is especially clear. People can try hard and still fail. They can make mistakes, sin seriously, and find they have ruined what they thought at the outset was a shining love. What do we do with them, for them, when their marital love has failed? Obviously, we should not abandon them, because that would be to act contrary to our God. We should search with them for ways to clean up as much of the mess as we can. Practically, emotionally, spiritually, morally, we should help them find ways to repair as much of themselves as they can. In a word, we should offer them the challenging, healing love of Christ. They must repent of their sins and pledge themselves not to abuse love in the future. They must not despair, must not stop believing God can make all things new. And we must let them teach us about our own sinfulness, vulnerability, temptations to despair. The only right, Christian, ethical way to handle divorce is for all of us, the full Christian community, to deal as realistically and lovingly as we can with the challenges it puts to our faith.

Abortion

In a manageable chapter of a book published after *Our Right to Choose*, her important work on abortion, Beverly Wildung Harrison deals masterfully with the issues involved in the theology and morality of procreative choice. She indicates the role that misogynism has played in the development of Western attitudes toward procreation, suggests some of the historical variability in the Church's understanding of abortion, and takes the discussion of the morality of abortion away from a single-minded focus on the act itself, so as to account for the full social reality that women making decisions about abortions have to face.

Toward the end of her essay, when she is starting to summarize her argument and suggest implications for political tactics and social policies, Harrison writes:

A feminist position demands social conditions that support women's full, self-respecting right to procreative choice, including the right not to be sterilized against our wills, the right to choose abortion as a birth control means of last resort, and the right to a prenatal and postnatal health care system that will also reduce the now widespread trauma of having to deliver babies in rigid, impersonal health care settings. Pro-lifers do best politically when we allow them to keep the discussion narrowly focused on the morality of the act of abortion and on the moral value of the fetus. We do best politically when we make the deep connections between the full context of this issue in women's lives, including this society's systemic or patterned injustice toward women.

It is well to remember that it has been traditional Catholic natural law ethics that most clarified and stressed this distinction between the morality of an individual act on the one hand and the policies that produce the optional social morality on the other. The strength of this tradition is probably reflected in the fact that even now most polls show that slightly more Catholics than Protestants believe it unwise for the state to attempt to regulate abortion. In the past, Catholics, more than Protestants, have been wary of using the state as an instrument of moral crusade. Tragically, by taking their present approach to abortion, the Roman Catholic hierarchy may be risking the loss of the deepest wisdom of its own ethical tradition. By failing to acknowledge a distinction between the Church's moral teaching on the act of abortion and the question of what is a desirable social policy to minimize abortion, as well as overemphasizing it to the neglect of other social justice concerns, the Roman Catholic Church may well be dissipating the best of its moral tradition.[11]

I find these paragraphs stimulating indeed, though not everything that Harrison proposes convinces me. First, there is the matter of women's full, self-respecting right to procreative choice. What goes into this right, and what restricts it?

Procreation occurs in the bodies of women, so clearly women have certain primary rights to control it. For men, or other women, to force given women to procreate against their will would be tantamount to rape. Even though many patriarchal codes have whittled away the moral affront of rape, it remains utterly prohibited in authoritative Christian ethical teaching. The same, I believe, with compulsory procreation. Morally, women can neither be forced to procreate nor be forced to forego procreation. Their assent is a fundamental condition for any good, moral act concerning their fertility.

Second, does this rightful procreative autonomy of women extend to the right to choose abortion as a birth control means of last resort? Here matters become more complicated. Is there a qualitative difference between birth control means of less than last resort and abortion? Most commentators would say yes. Do men, especially husbands, have important rights concerning procreation and abortion? Inasmuch as they are necessary for procreation, and ought to have a stake in the raising of children, surely they do. What about the rights of the fetus? Does it make sense to think of the fetus as innocent human life with a right to develop to birth? Reams of paper have gone into the discussion of this issue, which I'm certainly not going to resolve tidily in a few sentences here.

The persuasion of the pro-life position lies in the evidence it can bring forward that fetal life is distinctively human and that our most human instincts run to protecting it as such. The specifically Christian depth of this position is that human beings, perhaps from early development in the womb, have the dignity of being at least potential partakers of the divine nature. Harrison is right in saying that the strength of those opposing abortion comes from their clear, narrow focus on the reality of the fetus and its human rights. Can one kill something so human simply because it would be born at a bad time, into undesirable circumstances, with painful consequences for other family members and, perhaps, society at large? That seems dubious.

How much should the patterns of injustice against women weigh in our moral configurations of abortion? Is what Harrison calls the traditional Catholic wisdom of distinguishing between the private and the public aspects of a moral issue like abortion fully applicable in this case, or are the Catholic bishops more attuned than Harrison to the traditional wisdom of their Church in deciding that abortion is not so optional a matter as others where the distinction can serve well?

I find it easy to multiply questions like these, and hard to come to firm, crisp conclusions. I agree that the most desirable social policies would minimize abortions (and so would entail contraception and sex education). I am moved by other sections of Harrison's essay where she makes it plain that she thinks no responsible women consider abortion desirable. Thus much in my struggle to find my own position on abortion amounts to weighing the factors that, by the consensus of reputable commentators like Harrison, have to show up in any responsible treatment.

I find a strong desire to block out the ideology that both right-to-lifers and pro-choicers have developed (becoming more strident and polarized in the years since Harrison wrote this essay). "Abortion rights" have become powerful symbols. Ironically, I find them symbolizing the failures of both radical feminists and repressive Church people. What in another context[12] I have called "the double cross" that radical feminism and misogynistic Christianity can create comes back to me now. In opposing the right to abortion on demand, I feel I am honoring my Christian conscience. But I worry that I am also fueling the sexism of the Christian Churches. So my first instinct is to distance myself as much as possible from the noise of the ideologues on both sides.

My second instinct is to lament the dearth of treatments that pay equal attention to the actual circumstances in which women now contemplate abortions and the call of God to live differently from the world. Those actual circumstances run the gamut from heroic love to stunning selfishness. Some abortions are truly contraceptions of last resort, while others are a second or third operation to clean up acts, even relationships, indefensibly careless. Also, the call of God can be extremely demanding at times, though I think we are foolish to paint God as the enemy of common sense.

So, the people I most admire are wrestling constantly with both these matters, both these dimensions of the moral issue of abortion. They have not reduced the tension by aligning themselves unequivocally with "the feminist" or "the religious" camp. They feel a strong need to keep thinking, keep praying. I find much evidence that Beverly Harrison has kept thinking about abortion, as about many other demanding social questions. In this article I find less indication than I would like that she has struggled to hear God's voice directly, through prayer, but perhaps the genre of her piece (a polemical essay) makes that understandable.

Is my drift to let people make up their consciences as their illuminations at prayer and their individual circumstances suggest? To some extent, yes. But not completely so, because I am not convinced that abortion is so private as that would suggest — not convinced that abortion can by its nature be left to only what the people directly involved find best. Uniquely, the fetal "other" ineluctably involved in the act of abortion has claims to be heard, respected, let live. Even if its parents should think the termination of the pregnancy best, the child in the womb has independent interests that should be taken into account.

Can we ask an innocent pre-person to cede its right to life without demur? At what stage of a pregnancy does the fetus become someone apart from its mother, a person in its own right? Once again, I find questions such as these difficult. The moment of viability, or even of quickening, seems to mark a divide from the moment of conception and the first months of development, but gestation may well be a continuum. On the other hand, the later, larger fetus seems to possess more rights than the fetus of the first trimester, and so both to require less permission from its mother to survive and to allow its mother less freedom to abort it as she wishes.

The social aspects of an unwanted birth introduce another important factor, both complicated and vitally significant. Feminists are right to demand that we consider the twenty years or so for which the mother — ideally the whole family — will be caring for the child. Poverty, drugs, the possibility of adoption, child abuse, education, health care — what social factors can be disregarded in good conscience? The only responsible answer is none, but I don't find this answer to entail unabridged rights to choose abortion.

Perhaps my difference from most feminists at this point comes from my traditional philosophical training. To my mind, the being of the child is more basic than the well-being of its parents. What this metaphysical judgment ought to imply for policy questions remains uncertain, something yet to be worked out, but I have to pause before simply eliminating the being of the fetus, for reasons that most other feminists seem not to entertain.

Even when they have fine emotional sensitivity, are alert to every horrible implication of what is often a no-win situation, most feminists tend to be pragmatists, not persuaded that an objective order, ultimately derived from God, inheres in our evolutionary world of space and time. Nowadays, most feminists have no conceptual framework by which to justify any absolute rights — for instance, entitlements that a fetus, a human being in the womb, might accrue simply by being. Rather, most feminists think rights must be earned by participation in society, or, in the case of the fetus, must be subordinate to those of the mother and others who have come to human maturity.

The real affront of the traditional theory of natural law is that this law participates in the eternal law of God that structures creation. Such a conception falls outside the secular pale. For secularists, God is not something constitutive of the human makeup. Their sense of what it means to be human does not flow constitutively from a capacity to know God, love God, and serve God — from a capacity inseparable from human spirituality (our having the ability to know and love at all). What the status of this orientation to God is for the fetus, or even for the small child, is hard to determine. Still, the small child is nothing if not a bundle of desires to know and love, while the more we learn about life in the womb, the less we can distinguish the fetus from the small child.

So my tentative practical conclusions about abortion are the following: force right-to-lifers to confront the full social circumstances in which actual abortions are occurring; ask pro-choicers to back away from their solipsism, which often wants to exclude God, as though God were not what most constitutes our humanity; defend the interests of the fetus as though it were somewhat independent of its parents, because it is; grant women a positive bias in all discussions of abortion, because women have been slighted in the past and nowadays usually have the most acute sense of the actual choices involved; reconcile oneself to the imperfections of the world in which God apparently asks us to live, and so keep oneself from fanaticism of any kind; work for the wholesale changes in culture and values that a truly just society, fully hospitable to children, women, poor people, and people from minorities, implies; and, perhaps most importantly, spend more time with children, to realize better how miraculous they are, as well as how much we pledge them when we presume to bring them into our twisted adult world.

⨳ 5 ⨳

Ecclesiastical Issues

Scriptural Problems

In this chapter our topic is ethical issues deriving from membership in the Christian assembly, the Body of Christ. However loyal feminists may be to the Christian assembly, however grateful for its mediation of divine life, simple honesty requires most to charge that the Church has been part of the problems that women have faced during the past two thousand years. Indeed, the sexism of the Churches continues to be a major stumbling block today. The Church regards the Bible, both testaments of Scripture, as its constitution. We may begin, therefore, with ethical problems posed by Scripture itself.

On the first page of her provocative book on some Old Testament narratives problematic for women, Phyllis Trible confronts the matter of telling sad stories:

In this book my task is to tell sad stories as I hear them. Indeed, they are tales of terror with women as victims. Belonging to the sacred scriptures of synagogue and Church, these narratives yield four portraits of suffering in ancient Israel: Hagar, the slave used, abused, and rejected; Tamar, the princess raped and discarded; an unnamed woman, the concubine raped, murdered, and

114

dismembered; and the daughter of Jephthah, a virgin slain and sacrificed.

Choice and chance inspire my telling these particular tales: hearing a black woman describe herself as a daughter of Hagar outside the covenant; seeing an abused woman on the streets of New York with a sign, "My name is Tamar"; reading news reports of the dismembered body of a woman found in a trash can; attending worship services in memory of nameless women; and wrestling with the silence, absence, and opposition of God. All these experiences and others have led me to a land of terror from whose bourn no traveler returns unscarred. The journey is often solitary and intense. In joining this venture, the reader assumes its risks.[1]

The texts that Trible subjects to thorough literary scrutiny are Genesis 16:1-16, 21:9-21; 2 Samuel 13:1-22; Judges 19:1-30; and Judges 11:29-40. In laconic, chillingly simple language, they display rejection, rape, wanton abuse, and murder, epitomizing the fate of the myriad women throughout history who have had the misfortune to run into wicked men. Moreover, Trible's opening orientation makes it clear that her study is no venture in detached scholarship. The abuses detailed in these scriptural texts continue to occur in our cities and towns today. All over the world women continue to be subject to the whims of violent men, who beat them, rape them, even murder and dismember them, when rage or caprice makes such behavior seem good. Only the most obtuse reader could miss the point: Does what one sees in these biblical narratives function as a paradigm, if not a sanction, for the violence visited on women through history in the cultures that harken back to the Bible? What responsibility do the authors of the Bible, the God of the Bible, bear for the blood streaming from the flesh of women battered and ruined by men?

Such comfort as Trible can provide is cold and minimal, though perhaps by her own reckoning enough. Using the story of Jacob's wrestling with an unknown force, perhaps divinity itself, at Jabbok (Genesis 32:22-32), she muses:

> The fight is close to an even match. As Jacob prevails, the man puts out of joint the hollow of Jacob's thigh. Their physical struggle yields to a verbal contest, with Jacob refusing to let the man go unless he blesses him. The night visitor deflects this demand by eliciting a confession of the name Jacob as trickster, cheater, or supplanter. To reorient the identity of the patriarch, he changes that name to Israel ("God rules"). But again, Jacob wants to trick the assailant. "Tell me, I pray, your name," he asks. Although the request demonstrates a continuing desire for power, it is defeated by an all-knowing question, "Why is it that you ask my name?" Only then does the powerful opponent bless the mighty striver. What Jacob wants, he does not get on his own terms. The outcome acknowledges both the crippling victory and the magnificent defeat of that night. Jacob's life is preserved, but he limps as he leaves the Jabbok.
>
> As a paradigm for encountering terror, this story offers sustenance for the present journey. To tell and hear tales of terror is to wrestle demons in the night, without a compassionate God to save us. In combat we wonder about the names of the demons. Our own names, however, we all too frightfully recognize. The fight itself is solitary and intense. We struggle mightily, only to be wounded. But yet we hold on, seeking a blessing: the healing of wounds and the restoration of health. If the blessing comes—and we dare not claim assurance—it does not come on our terms. Indeed, as we leave the land of terror, we limp.[2]

Among the prestigious figures that a feminist reading can hold responsible for the injuries done to women in these Old Testament texts stand Abraham and David. The patriarchal slant on women that makes abuse commonplace, though not justified, warps both these heroes' personalities. They do not defend Hagar and Tamar as simple justice, let alone compassion for women's vulnerability, tells us they should. They are part of the violent male culture from which biblical women could suffer at a moment's notice. In taxing them with guilt, one is saying that biblical culture itself is unacceptable — by both today's feminist standards and its own better ideals. In taxing them with guilt, one is moving close to taxing God, who bears some responsibility for the evolution of biblical culture, as for all human cultures. That is the depth of Trible's challenge: Where is God in the suffering of women? Why should it have to be enough to limp away with a dubious blessing, given on terms we can barely recognize? Worse, why have so many women not even been able to limp away — been raped to death like the unnamed woman in Judges 19, been tortured, burned, and dismembered like countless Latin American women in recent decades?

The ethical question lurking here is whether it is moral to commit oneself in faith to the God proposed by the biblical communities, both Christian and Jewish. The only way to justify an affirmative response is to find evidence that God does more good than harm, provides more help than hindrance. We all have to make up our own minds on this matter. No one can believe for us. Healthy ethics does not value the merely pragmatic or utilitarian. "More good than harm" is not counted out in terms of money or power, even in terms of pain or joy. Healthy ethics values things in terms of meaning: Does clinging to the biblical God give our lives more sense, more possibility, than rejecting the biblical God? In specifically feminist terms, does clinging to the biblical God make it better to be a woman than rejecting such a God does?

I believe the crux of the Christian feminist ethical response to this question lies in the matter of grace, God's life. If one finds that the life of God revealed through the biblical texts and made available through the prayers and activities of the biblical communities takes one's own life up into new realms, into transcendent areas of meaning and repair that remain unrecognized apart from faith, then one can justify faith in this God — indeed, cannot justify holding back from faith. Trible hints at the possibility that God is our main argument against God's own deficiencies. The terms — on which the blessing that lets us think being human as either women or men is supportable—are the terms God chooses, not our own.

In the Christian case, which Trible does not illumine, those terms include the cross of Christ. For reasons we cannot fathom, God has chosen to make suffering like that of Jesus the way to redemption. The arguments of apologists soon fall by the wayside. The real ethical struggle is the one we can only live through day by day. The glory of the biblical literature is its honesty about this struggle for faith. The writers of Genesis, 2 Samuel, and Judges, like the writers of the New Testament depicting Christ's passion, force us to challenge God to own up to the evil in God's world. Feminist ethicists can only remain in the Church, be fully Christian, when they can say that the passion, death, and resurrection of Christ more than overbalance the evil done to women in God's world—in fact, overcome it. That proposition may seem obvious, nearly a deduction from the simple meaning of the terms *Christian, feminist,* and *ethicist*. The benefit of books like Phyllis Trible's is that they compel us to mind our speech. Unless we see the audacity of biblical faith, we remain shallow Christians whose support of feminist ethics carries little weight.

In a challenging series of reflections on the Gospel of Mark, novelist Mary Gordon shows the difficulties faith runs into when it has not settled the matter of what God has accomplished through Jesus. Gordon comments on Mark 7:24-30:

> A Gentile woman comes to beg Jesus to drive the evil spirit out of her daughter. He says to her, "Let the children be satisfied first, it is not fair to take the children's bread and throw it to the dogs." The interpretation of this cruelty from the altar [in the preaching that Gordon heard growing up] was that Jesus was testing her to show the greatness of her faith. But it also could be simple xenophobia. He thought originally that He was preaching to Jews. She beats Him on His own linguistic grounds. "Sir, even the dogs under the table eat the children's scraps." She bests Him using the technique He uses against the Pharisees: turning His own words against Him. But what a time for word play: who would

say this to a mother, distraught over her child's possession?

She seems, however, to be one of the importunate women from whom Jesus learns. He sends her home; her daughter is cured. He has taken his first step in allowing the world outside the Law of Moses into the Kingdom.

We were never allowed to think of Jesus as someone who learned, or grew or developed. Particularly in relation to a woman.[3]

In introducing her study Gordon has been winningly honest about the difficulties the gospels have presented her. However, throughout her remarks, as in those we quoted, a bitterness toward the Catholic Church of her youth plays like a leitmotif. I believe that her feelings are more justified than not, if one stays on the level of ordinary parish life. Compared to what a sophisticated person knows and needs nowadays, the presentations of faith standard in the majority of parishes thirty years ago fail miserably. What Gordon does not touch, though, is the real center of the gospel message (and the real center of the Catholic liturgy), which not even the mediocrity of the average parish could obliterate.

Jesus does help the Gentile woman. He may indeed have learned from her. Explaining this, at the core of Mark and the other gospels, is the conviction that what Jesus did for all those whom he encountered, and what Jesus learned through his sufferings, accomplished the radical liberation of humanity from sin, death, and meaninglessness. For Mark, Jesus is the Son of God, because the way that Jesus died, and rose, bore the signature of God. Everything has changed in consequence of Jesus, including the consciousness of women subjected to fears and sufferings like those of the Gentile mother, even like those of Hagar, Tamar, and their sisters mutilated throughout history.

Christian feminist ethicists can only pass judgment on the adequacy of the biblical God when they enter into a conversation with the biblical text that allows the gospels to be what they claim: good news. Until that point, both praise and blame are superficial. If Jesus has done what no one other than the Son of God could, all problems and difficulties shift dramatically. They do not go away, but we are bound to think and feel about them differently, utterly hopefully. If God has not accomplished in Jesus the eschatological victory, the definitive work of salvation that makes no suffering, no matter how horrible, meaningless, then we are bound to find Christian ethics of any stripe false and irrelevant. If God has accomplished in Jesus the definitive work of salvation, then all sufferings, including those of abused women, are penultimate—tears that believers can be certain God will wipe away from their eyes on the day when death will be no more.

Resistance to Women in Official Circles

In a study of how women like the Gentile mother appear in the lectionary (the collection of scriptural readings to be used in the liturgy), Marjorie Proctor-Smith documents the marginalization of female actors in the drama of salvation. Concerning the materials from the gospels themselves she writes:

Since even the Gospel texts themselves reflect the active presence of the faithful women disciples in particular during the events leading up to Jesus' death, the lectionary's treatment of them is of special interest. They appear in some of the readings for Passion Sunday, Monday of Holy Week, Good Friday, Easter Vigil, and Easter Day, but the inconsistency with which texts referring to the faithful women are used reveals that the compilers tended to regard them as peripheral rather than central to the action. For example: it is clear that in both Mark and Matthew the anointing of Jesus' head by the unnamed woman in whose memory the action is to be retold (Matt. 26:6-13; Mark 14:3-9) is the beginning of the passion narrative. Similarly, the women—named this time—mark the end of the passion narrative, as witnesses: they "saw where he [Jesus] was laid" (Mark

15:47; see Luke 23:55, Matt. 27:61). Yet the lectionary includes the anointing story only in the longer reading for Passion Sunday of Year B, when Mark's account is read; it does not include it at all in Year A when Matthew is read, and even in Mark's account it may be omitted when the shorter reading is used. The women's witness at the entombment may also be omitted in Years A and B if the shorter reading is to be used. In Year C the women's witness to the crucifixion is retained. It is interesting to note that although all three synoptic Gospels mention the women as witnesses to the crucifixion (as well as the entombment), only Luke places the women in the larger company of all of Jesus' acquaintances, and only Luke's text is included in the shorter passion readings. The Matthean and Markan accounts, which single out the women, are cut off, for the short reading, at the preceding verse. Evidently the women's role was not regarded by the compilers as essential to the proclamation of the passion and death of Jesus. . . . It is evident that the lectionary's hermeneutical principles fail to take women seriously as active, significant agents in salvation history. They are regarded as adjuncts to male actors, they are important in relation to marriage; otherwise they are expendable.[4]

Here the issue is not the place of women in the Bible, problematic as that may be. The issue is how the Church has refocused the New Testament's picture of women through its selections of the scriptural passages to be used in public worship. Proctor-Smith contends that the process of selection evidences a bias against the centrality of women.

The place of women in the New Testament is marginal enough. By the time that the lectionary has been composed, women are so far to the edge of the drama of salvation that one may wonder whether they had *any* significant role in Jesus' life or work. Unconsciously, one assumes, the (largely clerical) compilers of the liturgical readings have decreed that women could not be central players in the drama of salvation. One might need Mary, since Jesus had to be born from a woman, as all human beings are, and one could not deny the presence of women among Jesus' disciples. But one could omit texts dealing with women whenever reasons of space prompted curtailing the narrative. The patterns according to which Church officials tailored the lectionary suggest that the officials did not consider women as significant as men. The drama of salvation was a male affair. Women merely wept or believed on the sidelines, like cheerleaders at a football game.

We noted when dealing with Phyllis Trible's texts of terror that the Bible furnishes materials for questioning the role of God in women's fate. Earlier, we noted how Elisabeth Schüssler Fiorenza and Mary Hunt have raised questions about the acceptability of the biblical worldview for women. Here we may add that the New Testament itself offers the grounds that clerics have sought for challenging the marginalization of women. Even when one admits that the New Testament is the product of patriarchal cultures, and that some of the Pauline passages about women seem irredeemably sexist, the fact remains that Jesus stood out from the other rabbis of his day for his sympathies toward women. Indeed, the fact remains that Jesus made the poor, sinners, children, women, and the other powerless people of his day the prime citizens of the Kingdom of Heaven. He treated friends such as Mary and Martha as full disciples. He first appeared after the resurrection to Mary Magdalene, sending her to preach the good news of his triumph to Peter and the other disciples.

There are good grounds, then, for opposing Jesus to the compilers of the lectionary. Women were not so marginal to Jesus as the lectionary assumes and implies. The marginalization of women in the readings used for the official liturgy is the product of ecclesiastical sexism, not the product of Jesus' view of women. Church leaders have much of which to repent if they are to serve their Lord well concerning women's roles in redemption. As long as they continue to make women second-class disciples and believers, they stand in sinful opposition to Jesus, making it difficult for all feminists, men as well as women, to accept his offer of salvation.

Mary Collins has disclosed some of the historical and psychological dynamics underlying ecclesiastical sexism by speaking of a clerical "refusal" of women in Roman Catholicism:

> Refusal of women is a constitutive mark of the clerical circle, one of the ways clerics define themselves over against other baptized Christians and other human beings. It is essential to the self-definition of clerics that they name maleness as a primary qualification for incorporation into their circle, that they pledge themselves to restrict their associations with women, that they never marry one, and that they understand themselves, in any necessary relations with women, to be superior to them. If a quasi-authoritative article in the *New Catholic Encyclopedia* of the 1960s is to be trusted, associations with women are perceived to be high risk situations because of the consequences of loss of sexual control. That clerical writer notes that sins against the chastity of a cleric have the quality of sacrilege—the profaning of the holy, the desecration of the sacred.[5]

Behind this mentality lurks the hierarchical view of reality that ruled in the early days of the Church, when it was making its way into Hellenistic culture. The place of women in this hierarchical reality was the bottom rungs of the ladder, the base of the pyramid. God, a God of order, had decreed that men occupy the ranks of authority and power. In the Church the upper ranks belonged to clerics, all of whom had to be men. One might consider this merely historical information, testifying to the beginnings of Christian social life in Hellenistic society, did Church leaders not continue to perpetuate it today.

Indeed, as Collins notes, it continues to structure the training of priests and the ceremonies consecrating clerics, at critical junctures telling both them and the Church at large that women fall outside the structure of authority in institutional Christianity:

> The emergence of the clerical viewpoint is understandable as an event of human history, even if it is based on

a cosmological bias which invites cross-examination in the interests of achieving greater truth. How does the clerical world persist, and why? We cannot underestimate the role the institutions and rituals of the clerical ordo have played in the maintenance of the clerical worldview for clerics. The Roman Catholic seminary is one such institution which successfully inculcates this worldview; as such, it is a carefully protected institution. Young men predisposed to the clerical viewpoint for whatever reason are inducted into the Church's clerical ordo step and step [sic] and taught its ways. No curriculum attends to the matter explicitly, but the patterns of seminary life include overt and covert lessons on a necessary suspicion of women as sexual beings and of male superiority to them. Sometimes lessons in contempt have been taught.

Rites of ordination celebrate hierarchical relationships of higher and lower status, inferior and superior rank, and proclaim that all this is God's design. The consecratory prayer for the ordination of deacons declares: "Almighty God . . . you are the giver of preferments, the assigner of roles, the one who arranges official appointments . . ." Those who gather in solemn liturgical assembly for the ordination of presbyters hear it said of God: "[you are] the source of preferments, the one who assigns all ranks, the one through whom the whole world advances and everything is made secure."[6]

Needless to say, the hierarchical reality that God is said to create in the Church refuses to honor the equality of women central to the feminist agenda. As a good Christian feminist, Collins refuses to accept this refusal. Her argument is that one cannot serve both God and a sexist order or reality imposed in God's name. By implication, one has to reject the authority of those claiming that God requires a sexist, discriminatory arrangement of power in the Church. Further, one has to say that the essence of Christianity reposes in neither such a historically conditioned arrangement nor the clerical powers imposing it. The latter cannot be the sole, let alone the infallible arbiters of the divine will.

Technically, Collins does not infringe on the Roman Catholic doctrine of papal infallibility. No competent theologian would claim that clerical "preferments" have been defined *ex cathedra* to be an essential part of the Christian message, or even of the constitution of the Christian community. Politically, however, Collins throws down a gauntlet, one familiar to all readers of the history of ecclesiastical reform and dear to loyal Christian feminists today: the will of God is that we reform our sinful ways, in the present case the ways that have made our Church sexist. If forced to choose between this will of God (this specification of God's constant requirement that we do justice in love) and the images, even the orders, of clerical authorities, the alert believer can only follow the example of Saint Peter, the first pope, saying: "We must obey God rather than men" (Acts 5:29).

Women-Church

For some women, obedience to God rather than men means re-forming the Church into a community in exodus from patriarchal sexism. Rosemary Radford Ruether has described "women-Church" in these terms:

Israel and the Church, as communities of exodus from oppression and journey toward liberation, have been defined historically by males. Women have typically participated enthusiastically in the early stages of exodus movements and have believed themselves included in this liberation as *women* and not simply as adjuncts to a male project. The language of the exodus and the prophetic traditions which spoke of "Israel"; the language of the early Church which spoke of "brethren" as including all in a new humanity in Christ without regard to gender, ethnic group, or social station; the language of the Reformation and of modern liberation theologies all have led women to believe that they were included.

But, in fact, women have been betrayed by these male-defined projects of liberation. The male leaders of the exodus have set themselves up as a new ruling class of priests, ministers, and magistrates, politicians or party apparatchiks. In the laws of the new community of redemption, women have again been defined as subordinate or, at best, auxiliary to a male-defined social order.

Women-Church represents the first time that women collectively have claimed to be Church and have claimed the tradition of the exodus community as a community of liberation from patriarchy. This means that patriarchy is rejected as God's will. It is rejected as the order of creation or as a reflection of biological nature. Patriarchy is named as a historically contrived social system by which the "fathers"—that is, ruling-class males—have used power to establish themselves in a position of domination over women and also over dependent classes in the family and society. . . .

Thus the first step in forming the feminist exodus from patriarchy is to gather women together to articulate their own experience and communicate it with each other. Women assure each other that they really are not crazy, that they really have been defined and confined by systemic marginalization of their human capacities. They develop words and analysis for the different aspects of this system of marginalization, and they learn how to recognize and resist the constant messages from patriarchal culture that try to enforce their acquiescence and collaboration with it. Distressing as it may seem to males who imagine themselves sympathetic to feminism, this process of consciousness raising must necessarily have a separatist stage. Women have to withdraw from male-dominated spaces so they can gather together and define their own experience.[7]

The ethical crux of such a move is what it intends to accomplish and what fruits it actually brings forth. Like any other Christian project hoping to be ethical (to please God by acting rightly), the creation of women-Church has to be a work of love. It has to intend the fuller flourishing of human beings and the richer praise of God. Manifestly, it cannot only intend but actually accomplish both. If women withdraw in a spirit of love to heal wounds that have kept them from realizing their full potential, from praising God as they have wanted to in their best moments, and from serving their fellow human beings with full vigor, who can deny the rightness of their venture? If they do not become haters of men, even men by many titles their enemies (the sources of the patriarchal abuses that have wounded their humanity), but rather become better lovers, who could dispute the presence of the divine Spirit in their work?

Christianity has long sanctioned withdrawal from the status quo to improve one's love and service of God. Not only has the Church itself sometimes spoken of an exodus from sinful times and mores, but it has sponsored the life of the evangelical counsels, monasteries, times and places of retreat. Both men and women have found it legitimate to forego marriage, even forego the active life of serving their neighbors, to contemplate the goodness of God and pray for the radical healing of humanity's deepest sicknesses. Indeed, at many periods the Church has proposed this contemplative life in particular, and the life of the evangelical counsels in general, as the most perfect way to imitate Christ. So those calling for the creation of women-Church have much tradition on their side. Whenever a regnant culture has been experienced as oppressive, injurious to believers' faith, the Christian community has felt justified in urging people to withdraw from it, renew their strength, arm themselves so they might return to fight for its overthrow

Ruether herself casts a bleak eye on movements that become separatist permanently. If women have no desire to return to the human family at large, the entire body of women and men symbolized by the Church, they kick against the goad of reality. There is no scriptural justification for such separatism, and much in both Scripture and tradition condemns it. By and large, prior reformers have felt justified in calling Church leadership to repent of its sins and stupidities, sometimes in very sharp language. However, no reformers honored by the Christian community as a whole have ever set women against men, or men against women, to construct a community open only to a given sex. Certainly many male reformers have been misogynistic, in effect denying the full humanity of women and so proposing a community in which women would be second-class citizens. But the example of Jesus, the Pauline insight (Gal. 3:28) that in Christ there is neither male nor female, the account of the creation of humankind in Genesis, and a dozen other scriptural and traditional guidelines have militated against separatism. The earth is the Lord's and the fullness thereof. Any retreat from the fullness of humanity symbolized by the union of women and men is a denial of the sovereignty of the Lord.

Speculating further, I find myself wishing that more descriptions of women's liberation from patriarchal bondage would treat the existential burdens that patriarchy has intensified but not created. All the abuses visited on women by patriarchal subjugations are certainly prominent parts of the problem to which the grace of Christ is for believers the radical solution. All the denigrations of female sexuality, female intelligence, women's ability to exercise power profitably in either the Church or society at large, and women's ways of viewing reality are wounds, pains, effects of sin that the death and resurrection of Christ, the new life in the Spirit of Christ, have to heal and overcome. But women suffer from more than patriarchal abuses. We suffer as well from, we are threatened more profoundly by, death, ignorance, finitude, and sinfulness that we have to acknowledge as our own—that we cannot fob off on men.

Much as we may want to love God generously, we women know that laziness and self-centeredness get in our way, keep us failing God day after day. Much as we want to live forever, understand God completely, offer both our friends and our enemies pure love, we find that we cannot—that we simply are not good enough. To become good enough, we have to become partakers of the divine nature (2 Peter 1:4). And what can make us partakers of the divine nature but divinity itself? What, for Christian faith, is more significant than the divine love-life that Christ offers? This love-life, this grace, is immortality, holiness, forgiveness, and complete fulfillment all in one. It is the crux of what all human beings need and long for, women and men completely equal, and we find it most formally in the Church.

Women-Church will only do its full job when it serves this divine grace that is the crux of human fulfillment. It will only be more help than hindrance to the liberation of women when it makes Christ its center, makes the Trinity and grace the great treasures Christ offers. This is the perspective I think any ethicist claiming to be fully Christian must take.

The further question of how mediating the grace of Christ relates to the Body of Christ that has developed in history as the catholic (universal, whole) Church is more a matter of ecclesiology than of ethics. Suffice it to say here that at some point women-Church has to become a servant of the entire "Great Church," if it is to meet the charge that Christ has given his disciples. It cannot be joined as branch to vine without losing itself in the vine. If it wants to grow in discipleship to Jesus, it has to become part of Jesus' full Body. It also has to enter into Jesus' mission, which amounted to laying down his life for his friends—for any people opening their hearts to him. It cannot exist just for itself. It has to be more than women's way of finding themselves, let alone their way of chanting hymns to their own beauty. The beauty of any validly Christian community belongs to God.

In an interview in 1987, Joan Chittister suggested some of the ecclesiastical reforms that I believe a healthy feminist exodus into women-Church would target. For example, on the question of the ordination of women (a question extremely painful to many women belonging to Churches, such as Chittister's Roman Catholic Church, unwilling to ordain females), Chittister said:

> You cannot have a changed understanding of the notion of ministry for women until you have a changed understanding of the notion of the personhood of women. The question is simply, what is a woman for?

And the answer is not from biology. It's from Shakespeare. It's Shylock's answer in *The Merchant of Venice:* "If you prick us, do we not bleed? If you tickle us, do we not laugh? If you poison us, do we not die." The answer is, "I am fully human. Therefore, I am fully graced by God. Therefore, I am fully called by God."

When they baptize a woman they don't say, "Now we pour this slightly diluted water on this slightly diluted creature who will give us slightly diluted Christianity— or ministry or service—back." When they bring the girl up to confirm her, and she stands next to the little boy who is her peer and colleague in this great Christian moment, they don't tap him on the cheek and say, "You are confirmed to do battle for Christ our Lord and the spreading of the faith," and then look at her and say, "You are almost allowed to do battle for Christ our Lord in faith."

Someplace along the line, the effects of the sacraments are going to have to be able to be manifested in the ministries, as much for a woman as for a man. There's either something wrong with the present theology of ministry, or there is something wrong with the present theology of all the sacraments. If women qualify for baptism, confirmation, salvation, and redemption, how can they be denied the sacrament of ministry?[8]

How indeed?[9]

Women's De Facto Ministries

Although Christian women have often been denied orders, they have ministered effectively not only in their families and neighborhoods but also on the national scene. Too often we overlook the accomplishments of women inspired by their faith to labor for the good of their fellow citizens. For example, four paragraphs taken virtually at random from James Kenneally's history of American Catholic women leave little doubt that Christian education and faith inspired many women to address the great problems of late nineteenth- and early twentieth-century working people:

Maud O'Farrell Swartz, a printer who was educated in a European convent school, was recruited by the League [the WTUL: Women's Trade Union League] as a result of her campaigning in the Italian language for woman suffrage [sic] in 1912. From 1922 to 1926 she was president of the WTUL and served as secretary to the New York State Department of Labor from 1931 until her death. Like [Mary B.] O'Sullivan, she was also a resounding advocate of world peace and internationalism.

Described as a "feminine comet across the political sky," and called a vicious little pest by Ignatius Donnelly, founder of the Populist party, Eva MacDonald Valesh had been inspired as a child by Dominican nuns. She raised the concerns of "homeless, voiceless women, helpless to cope" in her lectures throughout the Midwest for the Knights of Labor, Farmers Alliance, and Populist party. As a newspaperwoman she continued to battle for justice by advocating enfranchisement and exposing employer exploitation. She was hired by the AFL as an organizer and writer for its paper the *Federationist* but quit when [Samuel] Gompers refused to put her name on the masthead. She continued to write pieces on reform and support social work and unionization. As a result of her disappointment at the hands of Gompers, she no longer emphasized unions as the major means of improving working conditions for women wage earners but stressed, instead, the importance of suffrage. This stance was in keeping with her nomination in 1888 for the Minneapolis school board, allegedly the first time a woman was so honored by a major party.

Also influenced by Dominican nuns was Agnes Nestor, who helped found the International Glove Workers Union, which she served in a national capacity from 1903 until her death in 1948. Nestor, who was quite devout, was also a member of the executive board of the WTUL and chaired the Committee on Women in Industry of the National Council of Catholic Women. Like other union leaders, she lobbied for protective legislation, supported settlements, and championed suffrage as a means of promoting justice for women workers.

Another parochial-school product was Julia O'Connor Parker, who went to work for the telephone company at age eighteen. A graduate of the WTUL's school for organizers, she was president of the Boston League from 1915 to 1918 and on the national executive board from 1917 to 1926. More important, she led a series of successful strikes as head of the operators' department (which she had helped form) of the International Brotherhood of Electrical Workers. Although married in 1925 and the mother of two daughters, Parker not only continued serving in the labor movement organizing for the AFL, but was active in the presidential campaigns of 1932, 1936, and 1940, serving in the labor division of the Democratic National Committee.[10]

While traditional theologians might demur at calling work such as this ministerial, a feminist ecclesiology is bound to do so. Women have tried to love God and their neighbors within the parameters available to them. With often amazing creativity, they have widened their roles as wives, mothers, nuns, teachers, nurses, factory workers, and politicians of various stripes, to give fuller scope to their talents and desires to serve. Within the Churches they have met all the calls made upon them, even while chafing at the restrictions patriarchal leaders have imposed. The result is a strong stimulus to rethink the meaning of Christian ministry. Any faith-filled, effective service ought to qualify as ministerial.

Ministers are those who serve the gospel of Christ, the Father who gave Jesus his mission, Christ himself, and poor people languishing like sheep without a shepherd. Ministers are those whose faith compels them to speak, write, organize, give succor, and pray for the coming of the Kingdom of God. Whatever the legitimacy of the distinction between laity and clergy in the Christian Church, it is clear that all believers are called to minister, each in his or her own way. Ministry, like missionary activity, is intrinsic to a healthy faith. One cannot have one's heart filled with the love of Christ and not be driven to try to share this treasure, to serve others Christ's good news. Faith is not for oneself alone. The Church does not exist for itself, but for the world. If women are vital members of the Church, they are bound to be ministers, missionaries, people afire with a desire to spread Christian faith. Any frustration of this desire, whether by Church officials or by women themselves, is immoral—contrary to the ethos of Christ.

Indeed, it is not hard to argue that to try to frustrate such ministerial activity makes one an opponent of God. The women Kenneally describes would not be denied their passion to make the world of laboring people a better place. Against countless obstacles, they found ways to raise people's consciousness, make people aware of what justice and mercy required. It is not accidental that many of them had received religious schooling. Along with their ABC's, they had learned that God makes us members of one another, brothers and sisters responsible for one another. And so they responded by trying to improve working conditions, living conditions, wages, educational opportunities, especially for women but in the long run for all people. Naturally, they were often impelled also by ethnic, economic, and social motives. Naturally, the labor movement beckoned to many of them as a way to help their own kind enter more fully into the American dream of prosperity and democratic citizenship. But this does not detract from the ministerial character of their activities. Whoever tries to make the world a better place in which to live is serving the will of the Christian God.

The tragedy of Christian patriarchy is that it has straitened the potential of so many women, frustrating their capacity and desire to make robust contributions to improving the world. The unethical character of much ecclesiastical understanding of ministry, past and present, shows in such a frustration of the imperatives encoded in women's faith. As soon as one admits that women are as fully human as men, and as fully Christian, most traditional objections to women's full participation in the ministries of the Church, the entire mission of the Church, become trivial. Nothing in the nature of women or the nature of Christian faith decrees that women cannot serve in all essential Christian works. From the altar to the organizing hall, women are as capable of serving the gospel as men. Thus, there is no valid reason why women should not be priests and bishops. Let the criteria of leadership in the Christian community be aptness, competence, a sense of being called by God and wanted by one's community, and the range of talent available to the Church for service doubles, because women draw nigh as the full equals of men.

Often I've reflected after meeting with a Christian group composed of both men and women that the natural leader of the group, the one with the most intrinsic, precisely religious authority, was a woman. Vividly on two occasions it struck me that a particular woman seemed a far more attractive candidate for bishop than the current officeholder in our diocese. The history of Christianity is replete with women who offered the Church amazing zeal, faith, intelligence, and charisma. From the labor movement to the huge parochial school system, the history of American Catholic women makes concrete this general pattern. When feminists complain about the marginalization of women in the Church, they illumine more than their own frustrations. In broader perspective the marginalization of women means the drastic reduction of the Church's ability to meet its God-given responsibilities, and so reveals its significant sins.

In the name of human traditions, man-made laws about celibacy and women's unsuitableness for ordination, Catholic Church leaders are now failing to meet their major God-given responsibilities. The primary obligation of those entrusted with care of the Catholic Church is to feed their flock—furnish their people Word and Sacrament, provide local liturgical assemblies where the people hear again the good news of salvation and receive the body and blood of Christ their Lord. The spectacular decline in vocations to the priesthood in the past twenty-five years has left the American Catholic Church and the Catholic Churches of Europe unable to meet this primary obligation. All signs are that Church leaders could change the situation virtually overnight if they admitted qualified women and married men to the priesthood.

The problem is not a lack of vocations. The problem is the current official understanding of the priesthood, the present papal theology of orders and ministry, is not credible. In my experience, most ordinary members of the American and European Churches simply do not believe that celibacy and maleness are requisite for effective priestly ministry. Most have rejected any necessary ties between masculinity and serving to the People of God the Word of God, the body and blood of Christ. Equally, most have decided that celibacy should be an option, determined by the charismatic gift of God rather than a prosaic canon law. And so, in effect, most first-world Catholics have repudiated their current leaders as impoverished in sacramental faith, unethical in sacramental practice.

Feminists have helped to clarify this crisis of credibility, but they have not precipitated it. The behavior of recent generations of priests has been the major cause. Such priests simply have not made the case that women and married men could not do an equally good, indeed often a superior, job. Moreover, the bishops' failure to feed the flock of Christ is rapidly becoming a great scandal, threatening to brand them culpably ignorant of their reason to be. Christian feminist ethicists ought to clarify this judgment and promote it, with all proper gentleness, because it greatly serves not merely their own cause but the cause of God. At the present juncture, rendering justice to women in the matter of Christian ministry is the most direct way for the Catholic Church to furnish its people the Word and Sacrament that are the marrow of ecclesiastical life. In pressing for the ordination of women, feminists are in the fortunate position of helping the community of Christ become its better self.

Women's Spirituality

In her 1985 Madeleva Lecture, Monika Hellwig went to the heart of what women have to offer Christian ministry and spirituality:

A most significant conclusion is certainly that as long as women are systematically excluded from ordination and from the institutionalized positions of leadership and decision-making in the Church, this has some advantages as well as the more obvious disadvantages. To be deprived of the power of domination, to have little or no access to bullying power, to be unable to compel or persuade by threat or use of institutional sanctions, is necessarily to be thrown back upon other resources. And that may well be to discover that divine power, the power of grace, is of a very different kind, effective inasmuch as it empowers and liberates human freedom— freedom for self-transcendence, freedom for true community with others, freedom for God and for God's purposes in creation and history. On the other hand, to have access to bullying power is inevitably to be sorely tempted to use it. But it is not Christ's way. Because of our Church organization, Christ's way to empowerment of human freedom to transcend is likely to be more immediately apparent to women.

Looked at positively, the characteristic possibilities for a spirituality of Christian women that can really make a Christian difference in a troubled world seem to be concerned particularly with prayer, compassion, solidarity and creative imagination. These are qualities and components which bridge the gap between the available models in the tradition of the past and the situation of contemporary women with their far greater access to positions of power and public persuasion. The opportunities are much enhanced for us in our own times, but the strictures under which our forebears worked seem in some ways to make the issues clearer. The question for us in our times is how to make the best use both of the wider scope offered to us and of the insight that we can derive from the past with the narrower scope that it offered to women.[11]

How good to hear a feminist theologian speaking about the power and ways of grace! The fact is that God's ways are not our ways. Isaiah makes this plain, and Phyllis Trible makes us see it when she reflects on the lessons of Jacob's wrestling with the mysterious stranger, to say nothing of the lessons latent in the stories of Hagar and Tamar. Hellwig is not opposed to the ordination of women. Far from it. But she is believer enough to trust that no situation is without its advantages, things that God can turn to divine account. Inasmuch as women have been prohibited from gaining institutional power in many of the Christian Churches, they have not been tempted to abuse institutional power. Indeed, their life on the margins of institutional power has taught them that the ways of God, the power of God, have to be different from bullying and coercion.

Of course, this is obvious if one reads the New Testament with any attention. Jesus goes to his death nonviolently. He compels no one to believe in his gospel. He can be caustic, angry, sarcastic about his enemies, but he is never a bully. As soon as anyone, man or woman, comes to him humbly, in manifest need, his heart goes out and he does all he can to bring the power of God to bear on the person's problem. The ways of Jesus are ways of love. If women's marginal status has taught them the superiority of the ways of love, it has not been all bad.

The question for women today, when political if not ecclesiastical power is more available, is how to retain the superiority of the ways of love while simultaneously taking advantage of chances to make significant institutional, economic, cultural, and political changes. We cannot despise the access of women to great practical, secular influence. To do so would be to deny the Incarnation of God's Word, which has made all human activity sacramental in principle. On the other hand, we have to be realistic about the impurities that tend to come when one begins to wield secular power. It is difficult to remain counter-cultural, true to the values and methods of Christ. If the way of grace is gentle persuasion, feminist politicians and theologians have to remain gentle in their persuasions. They have to continue to believe in the long run, the long haul. They must see the inadequacy of any commitments that do not come from freedom, that are not compatible with perceptions of the transcendence of God.

The transcendence of God is the hallmark of any genuine Christian spirituality. Only if God is truly God, ineluctably mysterious, can a feminist spirituality claim to be religious. Only if it shows how the transcendence of God has been enhanced by the Incarnation of God's Word in Jesus can any spirituality claim to be fully Christian. The great issue in human existence, for Christian feminist ethicists, is how to become conformed to Christ, structured by the divine love that gave him his inmost identity and made him nonpareil among the leaders of world history. If one does not think that he is nonpareil among the leaders of world history, one's Christianity is dubious. If one does not find in him the liberation of women in principle from all the biases and prejudices of patriarchal cultures, one's faith is not both Christian and feminist. And if one does not act on these thoughts and findings, to the praise of Christ *and* the advancement of women's liberation into full equality with men, one is not ethical. Those are the provocative conclusions to which meditation on Hellwig's lecture leads me.

In the final paragraphs of her study of faith and feminism in the Catholic Church, Sandra Schneiders comes to some equally provocative conclusions:

> At no time in history, except perhaps at the time of the Protestant reformation, has the Church faced a crisis of such proportions [as that represented by feminist demands for reform today]. However, the Protestant reformation involved a relatively small segment of the Church in the tiny theater of western Europe. Feminism involves over half the Church in every location in the world. All of the mothers of future Catholics are women and, despite the exclusion of women from orders, by far the majority of the Church's professional ministers are women. While not all Catholic women are feminists, time and historical process is on the side of rising liberationist consciousness, not on the side of oppressive ideology. The Church as institution cannot survive the final disillusionment of women although women, as

Church, can probably survive the demise of the patriarchal institution. The conclusion is that because the issue is in the arena of spirituality it must be taken with
utter seriousness. If anything is to be learned from the
Protestant reformation it is that when reform is urgent
it may be deferred but it cannot finally be avoided and
the price of deferral can be disastrously high. . . .

The feminism of Catholic women is both the Church's
ultimate and most serious challenge and its best hope
for a future worthy of its gospel roots. When the male
disciples of Jesus returned from the town of Samaria
where they had gone to buy lunch they found Jesus in
deep theological conversation with a woman. We are
told that they were shocked and could not imagine what
Jesus wanted from a woman or why he would bother to
talk to her. But they knew better than to challenge Jesus'
designs whose horizons were obviously well-beyond
their culture-bound ken. So the woman, like other apostles who left boats and nets and father and tax stall to
follow Jesus and announce the good news, left her water
jar and went off to announce Jesus and to present her
fellow townspeople with the only question that really
matters: "Can this be the Christ?" Women today are
asking this same question of the institutional Church.
Can you recognize in us, in our persons and in our
experience, the image of Christ, and will you choose to
act accordingly?[12]

I find Schneiders's question poignant in the extreme, and
I certainly hope that the institutional Christian Church, hearing the call of the Holy Spirit to come to its better self, will
answer it affirmatively, above all by moving to treat women
as the full equals of men. The only supplement I would offer
(to this treatment of where the spirituality of Christian feminists now stands) is a brief meditation on what the Church
itself actually is, and so on why women of faith can never
actually leave it, no matter how far they may separate themselves from its patriarchal institutions.

The Church of Christ is the continuance of Jesus in space

and time. However badly, simply by being visible the followers of Jesus who comprise the Church keep present in history the good news of the Reign of God, the glad tidings that the eschatological deed has been accomplished. In the measure that any people see the neediness of human beings, the profound distortions of history, they can sense that the Church of Christ is utterly essential to maintaining hope. The only absolute future for human beings is the living God, holy and always mysterious, and for Christian faith the most definitive demonstration of the nature, power, and intentions of the living God is the resurrection of Christ.

The Church was born from the resurrection of Christ, which of course cannot be separated from his death, Ascension and sending of the Holy Spirit. The Church is the community formed by the memory, the living presence that takes hold of one's entire sense of reality, of the life, death, and resurrection of Christ. The human leaders of the Church are significant, because in Christ God has shown that divinity takes human flesh, human space, human time, and, above all, human freedom seriously. But the human leaders are also not significant, because the memory and present reality of Christ that make the Church the Church render it indefectible simply by occurring.

If the gospel is preached, the last supper celebrated anywhere in the world, then the message that Christians believe is the sole thing necessary for human hope continues to exist. Simply by existing, the Church keeps present to human beings the unfailing power of divine grace. The story of Jesus' saving life, made contemporary in each eucharistic assembly, defeats the world, the flesh, the devil, all our temptations to despair. Let it simply occur and people have an absorbing alternative. No matter how stupid, the leadership of the Church cannot block the power of this hopeful reality that the Church both is and exists to proclaim.

If the Church merely exists, through the celebration of Christian Word and Sacrament, then the world can know that there is a community of salvation. If there is a community of salvation, then women and men can find a human, social place where a story powerful enough to heal their threatened imaginations, to cure their nearly mortally wounded spirits, sings praise to God without cease. In their understandable rush to change the Church from its sexism to a justice worthy of God, feminists ought not to overlook this quintessential nature of the Church, which none of its (our) sinfulness, no matter how painful, destroys.

This theological fact is no justification for delaying the delivery of full justice to women. It is no warrant for saying that women's pains are superficial or that the sexism of the Church does not do unimaginable harm to both women and men. But it is a salutary reminder that God accepts women, Christ enlivens women with the eternal life of the unbegotten Father and loving Spirit, whether or not Church leaders have the wit to see women as their sisters, their equals, their beloved in the embrace of Christ's Body. God is not defeated by our stupidity and evil. The glory of the Church is that the undefeatable God has chosen to make it (us) the definitive locus of the grace that gives women and men what they have been made to receive from eternity.

Models of God

Eternity is the abode of God, the mode of God's existence. Christian ethics can never wander far from the preeminent reality of God if it wants to retain its distinctive savor. God is mysterious, and all our names for God, all our conceptions of how God operates in the world, are frail, faltering analogies. The beginning of ethical order is the simple acknowledgment of God. Let human hearts really enshrine God as their primary value and most of their subsequent problems will be minor. Idolatry is the great disrupter of right order, as Islam eloquently proclaims. It is no small matter, then, for feminist theologians to work at reconceiving God, the better to provide for the divine primacy and for insights, like those hinted at by Hellwig, into how the grace of God works in human affairs.

In a section of her significant work on what theology ought to stress in an ecological, nuclear age, Sallie McFague treats of the healing proper to a God who is the lover of creation. She has already dealt with the reconceptions or deepened insights that attending to God as a mother might produce. Here the accent is on how a divine lover may be imagined to deal with a world needing considerable healing:

> The reason that God as lover wants the beloved world healed and made whole is his great love for it. A lover feels the pain of the beloved deep within himself and would undergo any sacrifice to relieve the pain. One way to understand the passion of Jesus of Nazareth is as the suffering that inevitably came to him in his fight against the divisions separating people from God and one another—the hierarchies, dualisms, and existence of outcasts. The passion or death is the passive side of his active ministry as healer of the sick, prophet of inclusive love, liberator of the oppressed. The passive side witnesses to solidarity of each with all: in the model of God as lover there are no healers that do not feel wounded, no liberators that do not experience oppression. This second, passive side must be seen as second: solidarity with the sufferings of the beloved is a permanent feature of the kind of love for the world implicit in the model of God as lover; nonetheless, if it is conceived as the primary feature of salvation, acceptance of the status quo and a romanticizing of suffering occurs. In our model, suffering is not salvific but it is inevitable: it is a risk incurred by all who confront evil by siding with those who suffer and are oppressed.

Who, then, are the healers and the liberators—the "saviors" of the world? The tradition says there is only one, Jesus Christ, who does all the work. This position made sense in a time that understood the one thing needful to be atonement for sins, ransom from the devil, or reconciliation with an angry God, but if the one thing needful is reunification of the shattered, divided world, there must be many saviors. Jesus of Nazareth, as paradigmatic of God as lover, reveals God's passionate, valuing love for the world. In his teachings, healings, and death he seeks to make the beloved whole and free through overcoming hierarchies and dualisms, healing bodies and spirits, suffering in solidarity with the outcast and the oppressed. But as revelatory and powerful as that life was and continues to be, it cannot stand alone as accomplishing salvation if salvation is seen as the piecing together of the fragmented body of the world in one's own time and place. That work must be done and done again, by many minds, hearts, hands, and feet.[13]

This is a moving, intelligent rendition of an attractive model for God. It evidences many concerns that feminists now bring forward, especially those bearing on healing the wounds of the ecosphere and, behind those wounds, the lacerated human consciousness that we call patriarchal or hierarchical. Moreover, it is a model confessedly indebted to Jesus of Nazareth, who serves as the paradigm of love for humanity if not for creation as a whole. So I find in it much to praise, much that brings me positive resonances. All the more so is this the case when I place the model of God as lover in the fuller context of McFague's essay, which treats the motherhood of God fully. In what way, then, is this theology inadequate, not fully Christian?

Much is semantic in my judgment, and yet even after I've admired McFague's careful language, her manifest effort to relate her conscientious reworking of Christian traditions to notions hallowed through the Christian centuries, I miss a forthright confession of Jesus' full divinity, which would set all subsequent considerations in a significantly different light.

If Jesus is fully divine, and fully human, as the Christian creeds and councils (presenting themselves as authentic, authoritative interpretations of original, New Testament Christian faith) have claimed, then the salvation that he accomplished was once and for all: universal, definitive, unique, nonpareil, eschatological, absolute (choose your adjective carefully, but feel free to praise the divine accomplishment without measure). A specifically Christian theology does not take the Incarnation that grounds the full divinity of Jesus as merely metaphorical, any more than it takes the

Trinity as simply one figure for God among many good, useful, imaginative constructs. Certainly we never get away from debts to the imagination. Certainly all our theological speech is at best analogical; God is always more unlike than like what we say about God. The union of flesh and spirit in Jesus ensures that all his words and deeds will be metaphoric, symbolic, mysteries in the limited sense of scenarios that we may visit again and again for nourishment.

However, for traditional Christian faith the symbols laid out in Scripture and tradition are privileged. More, they are real—the best indications we have of what divinity is actually like in itself and of how we have been saved. They do not stand on a par with Hindu, Buddhist, or Confucian symbols. They are not on the same level as the latest theological reinterpretations of what Christian faith ought to mean in the contemporary age. They are fonts of faith, consecrated resources and expressions, so they carry more authority than any private imaginings of the nature of God or the character of God's actions in the world ever could.

Christian theologians aware of their task in the Church and desiring to be faithful in carrying it out do not feel free to pass by the strict divinity of Jesus, the full Incarnation of the divine Word in Jesus, the real taking flesh that led to considering Mary the *theotokos*. These are not bits of nostalgia that we can leave aside when we take up the work of fashioning a contemporary Christian theology that would do justice to such pressing problems as ecological devastation, the threat of nuclear holocaust, the Shoah that stalked God's first chosen people, the Jews, or the historic shifts in the consciousness and status of women that led Schneiders to speak of an unprecedented crisis in Christian spirituality. We cannot make Jesus merely advisory when we consider the function of the divine love in the healing of the ills of creation and humanity. To do so would be to exempt ourselves from the priority of Christian *faith* seeking understanding, to elevate ourselves above the historical community of believers and presume to possess a private wisdom more discerning or valuable. If we are to keep faith with the Christian past, we have to accept the ontological centrality of Jesus as the enfleshment of divinity that gives both creation and redemption their structure.

Of course, there are many people other than Jesus who deserve our admiration, because they have given flesh to the divine love that works to heal the divisions of creation. In fact, Christianity has long honored the saints as exemplars of faith, and there is no reason not to honor Buddhist, Hindu, Confucian, and other non-Christian holy people, calling them saints also. There is no contradiction between making Jesus the absolute bringer of salvation, or the bringer of absolute salvation, and praising the Buddha as a sage with wonderful insights into the nature of suffering and the processes of liberation (indeed, the processes of salvation: the reception of divine life). But there is a contradiction between presenting a theology as Christian and not making Jesus its crux — not finding in Jesus the unique revelation of what God is like, what humanity might become through God's grace, and where salvation (utterly radical healing) has taken place.

McFague probably does not claim to be operating as a Christian theologian, at least in a traditional, confessional sense. Inasmuch as she does not, she avoids the contradiction I am proposing. However, if she does not she also loses the specific power of confessional Christian faith, which is to claim that Christ has in principle healed all of reality — made all things whole and new.

This claim is so basic in the New Testament that one cannot be a representative Christian thinker while avoiding it. From Paul's imagery of Christ as the second Adam to Revelation's paeans about God wiping every tear from our eyes and death being no more, the New Testament insists that with Christ a new creation has occurred. Indeed, it insists that human nature has been divinized. Compared to these insistences, McFague's probings of ecological healing and human renewal seem genteel, if not superficial. In themselves they are marvelous, much of what any alert spirit longs to hope for nowadays. But when one sets them in dialogue, or better dialectic, with the claims that launched the Christian movement, they fade to bloodlessness.

Christian feminists, like Christians generally, have to face the audacity of the claims at the roots of their tradition. If they try to avoid the scandal of Jesus, the unique "moment" that meant so much to Kierkegaard, they eviscerate the faith that the apostles, the disciples, the early martyrs, and the confessors through the ages have found completely transforming. The only full healing of human nature, and through human nature of the natural world, is its divinization. The only adequate response to the Christian tradition is to update its claim that God has remade humankind. McFague is right to move away from models of healing that present Jesus as mainly satisfying for human guilt before the judgment seat of God. But those are not the models at the core of traditional Christian theology.

As Eastern Orthodoxy especially has known, the core of traditional Christian theology is the complete fulfillment of human nature through its being taken into the being, the nature, the love and light and life of God. This begins, is accomplished at root, in the Incarnation. It continues, in a mode of illumination and further humanization, through the earthly, active, ministerial life of Jesus. It engages evil, all that opposes the holy life of God, in the passion and death of Jesus. And it bursts forth, fully revealed, in the resurrection. Women are the equals of men in inheriting this faith, this tradition, this incomparably powerful reception of what God has done through Christ (and so what must shape Christian theology from the outset). For women to forfeit such a birthright would be to substitute the metaphors closest to Jesus for a mess of potage.

❧ 6 ❧

Conclusion

Christology

We have been concerned with Christian feminist ethics: its constitutive marks, some of its recent preoccupations and forms, the ontological orientation it needs. In conclusion, let me articulate the sense I would most like the phrase *Christian feminist ethics* to bear.

The first word, *Christian*, is capital. There are many useful ethical statements. There are many feminist works on ethics that offer insight and encouragement. But I find the word *Christian* the most crucial in the phrase, because this word gives me my basic orientation in life. I desire to be formed by faith in the Christian God, hope in the Christian God, love of the Christian God—more than any other forces. I desire to make Christ my paradigm for what it means to be human—the model I try to match, with my life even more than my mind. Even though I fail these desires every day, they determine my scale of values. For me, Christian faith is more important than feminism, even as Christian faith makes feminism imperative. Equally, Christian faith is more comprehensive and profound than any mere ethics—secular, feminist, or Christian. What we are is more basic than what we do, even though we only show and shape what we are through what we do. Inasmuch as God is the alpha and omega of human existence, the faith through which we con-

147

template God, try to understand God, and try to serve God has to be our primary resource when it comes to discoursing on the good life.

Therefore, I have been at pains to make the depths of Christian faith bear on such issues as social justice and sexual morality, as well as on how women ought to be treated in the Church. Many of my criticisms of contemporary feminist ethicists have boiled down to a disappointment with what they say about Christian faith, how they render, or fail to render (by ignoring), the revelation I find God's greatest gift. Since that revelation is not a creed or a code for behavior, but a living person, Jesus of Nazareth, believed by his disciples to be the Christ, the specification of the first word in the phrase that I have been worrying in this book is Christological. What we understand Jesus to have been and done in the past, and to continue to be and do today, is all-important in constructing or evaluating a Christian ethics.

As a case study, let us examine some lines from Rita Nakashima Brock's *Journeys by Heart: A Christology of Erotic Power*:

> In moving beyond a unilateral understanding of power, I will be developing a christology not centered in Jesus, but in relationship and community as the whole-making, healing center of Christianity. In that sense, Christ is what I am calling Christa/Community. Jesus participates centrally in this Christa/Community, but he neither brings erotic power into being nor controls it. He is brought into being through it and participates in the cocreation of it. Christa/Community is a lived reality expressed in relational images. Hence Christa/Community is described in the images of events in which erotic power is made manifest. The reality of erotic power within connectedness means it cannot be located in a single individual. Hence what is truly christological, that is, truly revealing of divine incarnation and salvific power in human life, must reside in connectedness and not in single individuals. The relational nature of erotic power is as true during Jesus' life as it is after his death.

He neither reveals it nor embodies it, but he participates in its revelation and embodiment. And through its myriad embodiments and playful manifestations, we are led to take heart.

Heart—the self in original grace—is our guide into the territories of erotic power. Through that power we come to touch and be touched by, to transform and be transformed by all that is "the whole and compassionate being." But to come to that wisdom involves understanding the depth of the broken heart of patriarchy and its symbols. Christ, as the center of Christianity, will share in the patriarchal broken heart as long as it supports unilateral views of power. Feminism and Christianity can converge in love and justice if Christ can come to reveal erotic power. This feminist Christology, in being guided by heart, develops another way to understand Christ that will lead us away from the territories of patriarchy and into a world in which incarnation will refer to the whole of human life.[1]

What have we here? First, we have a poetic writer, gifted at taking familiar words and weaving them into a quilt with new, feminist designs, a song with new, feminist emotional overtones. Second, we have a view, a version of Christology, probably impossible to square with traditional Christian doctrine, let alone traditional Christological dogma. Third, we have a priority of feminism over Christian faith—a subordination of Christian faith to feminist insights, intuitions, needs, desires. So, fourth, we have a saltus, a leap from the main branch of Christian evolution. Interestingly, it is a sport that significant numbers of Christian feminists find intriguing, even if they do not subscribe to all its features. However, do they realize what they are sacrificing if they decide to take it up as their orthodoxy—to model the play of God in their own lives after it?

It is not difficult to see why Brock's Christology should get a sypathetic hearing in feminist circles. Women who find traditional Christian doctrine or current Church life alienating are hungry for alternatives, new visions and communities that will be more congenial. They are tired of being treated as the second sex. Sexism, sinful prejudice against them as women, has worn them down, so they find it hard to resist a Christology that replaces patriarchal biases with notions dear to women: wholeness, relationality, erotic power.

I do not quarrel with Brock's stress on erotic power. Love is the force that moves the stars, for God is love. The distinction between agape and eros has broken down, and for good reasons. It makes more sense of both Scripture and human experience to say that God desires us—indeed, that God's desire for us is the ground of our goodness—than to say that God is completely selfless in loving us and our world. Certainly notions such as desire and selflessness, when applied to God, give us difficulties. They are clumsy tools, blunt instruments, for dealing with a love that we can barely glimpse. But the ardor of the biblical God, joined with the clearly transforming power of erotic love in our own lives, makes it clear that we have to retain eros when speaking of both how God loves the world into being, healing, and forgiveness, and what the divine life itself is most like. Thus, in demanding that Christology come to focus in erotic love and power, I think Brock is on the mark.

I think that Brock misses the Christian mark, however, when she makes erotic love and power the judge of Christ, rather than making Christ the judge of erotic love and power. Relatedly, I believe that she errs by thinking that "Christ" can be separated validly from Jesus of Nazareth. My understanding of Christianity makes both these moves unacceptable.

In the measure that we are Christian, we submit to the designs of reality revealed by God through Jesus the Christ. We do not presume to change these designs, making them unrecognizable. Certainly the large question of interpreting what God's designs actually are raises sizeable difficulties. As well, it endows theologians, people seeking to understand their faith, with considerable freedom. Yet the consensus of the Christian community through time, as well as the configuration of the main Christian symbols and articles of faith in worship, provides necessary guidelines. My sense is that

Brock has ignored these guidelines and so run afoul of what is recognizably called Christian.

I admire any effort to rethink the significance of Jesus for our day. I appreciate every effort to bring the old Christian convictions alive by connecting them with new senses of vitality, especially any effort that is poetic. On the other hand, I do not believe that patriarchy has vitiated the Christian message in the past, nor that it vitiates that message today. I do not find the Church's biases against women to have been a complete frustration of its mission to mediate divine life. God is "skillful in means," as the Buddhists say. The circumstances in which we find ourselves always contain enough of the solutions to our existential problems to allow us to give God a blank check—a confession that we are the pots, not the potter.

Women give birth and die. Women exult and weep in frustration. Women need food for their spirits as much as their bodies. The world is as mysterious to women as it is to men. Most relevant, in the present circumstances, women hunger for love, sense that love is the best index of God. Looking upon Jesus, meeting him in prayer and communal living, intuiting his presence in the poor, the sick, the emotionally distressed, women often feel touched by the finger of God— stirred to their marrow. These are experiences of the erotic power of God. The sufferings of Jesus himself purify our images of this power, even as they teach us how deeply we need a new creation worked by divine love. I cannot believe, because I do not experience, that Christa/Community is a rational substitute for Jesus the Christ.

What mature Christian thinks that women, no matter how well bonded by relationship, are better lovers, less sinful friends, than Jesus? What saints, female or male, would subscribe to such a proposition? Can one imagine hearing it from the mouth of Julian of Norwich, Catherine of Siena, Teresa of Avila, Therese of Lisieux, Mother Teresa, or Dorothy Day? Moreover, does not the sanctity of these Christian women call into question any writing them off as dupes of patriarchy— any dismissing their witness as that of people so oppressed that their humanity became ugly? Certainly many things were wrong in the Church of their day, including many offenses against women. None of these wrongs, however, kept them from finding in Jesus the key to absolute fulfillment.

Do we want absolute fulfillment, or are we willing to settle for a sisterly circle? Is there no difference between the holy otherness of God, from which Christians believe the definitive solution to our problematic human condition comes, and the congenial familiarity of like-minded human friends? A sisterly circle, like the blessing of like-minded friends, is part of God's hundredfold gift to us. But I subordinate it radically to the heart of the Christian matter, which is a love fully divine and thus the judge of human erotic love and power, not something these so fallible forces can judge.

In the final analysis, what I would call healthy, defensible Christology boils down to whether or not Jesus is unique in human history, because he was and continues to be the sole complete Incarnation of the divine Word, the sole human being so perfected by God's love that he became the absolute savior: the personal place where a new creation occurred. I believe that Christianity stands or falls by this claim, and that not to agree to it is to reduce Christology to psychology. Indeed, not to make or accept it is, in my view, to denature Christianity and opt for a wisdom and love so much lesser that, to do so knowingly, deliberately, would be completely unethical.

Womanist Ethics

In a helpful introduction to a roundtable discussion of Christian ethics in womanist perspective, Cheryl J. Sanders has shown considerable sensitivity to the question of how traditional Christian faith and Christology ought to relate to womanist convictions. Defining the term *womanist* as, in essence, "black feminist," Sanders first describes its connections to the novelist Alice Walker, who coined it, and to admirable black women, such as Rebecca Jackson, who were pioneers on the womanist path of taking personal experience as black women seriously enough to challenge whatever seemed to block the delineations of reality and personal destiny such experience revealed. Then Sanders enters a paragraph of caveats about what she fears are reductionist or secular readings of womanism:

> It is problematic for black women who are doing womanist scholarship from the vantage point of Christian faith to weigh the claims of the womanist perspective over against the claims of Christianity. The womanist perspective ascribes ultimate importance to the right of black women to name our own experience; in the Christian perspective, Christ is the incarnation of claims God makes upon us as well as the claims we make upon God. While there may be no inherent disharmony between these two assertions, the fact remains that there are no references to God or Christ in the definition of womanist. For whatever reason, christology seems not to be directly relevant to the womanist concept. And if we insist upon incorporating within the womanist rubric the christological confessions of black women of faith, or discerning therein some hidden or implicit christology, then we risk entrapment in the dilemma of reconciling Christian virtues such as patience, humility and faith, with the willful, audacious abandon of the womanist. Walker only obscures the issue by making vague references to the spirit instead of naming Christian faith and practice. For example, she uses terms like general power and *inner spirit* to describe Rebecca Jackson's motive for leaving husband, home, family, friends and Church to "live her own life." Yet it seems obvious that Jackson would name her own experience simply as a call to follow Christ. I suspect it is Christianity, and not womanism, that forms the primary ground of theological and ethical identity with our audacious, serious foremothers.[2]

Katie G. Cannon, responding to Sanders, shows the hot emotion that questions such as these can stir:

> In preparing to write this response, I found myself repeatedly stopped by waves of anger at Dr. Cheryl

Sanders' treatment of womanist as a secular terminolog-
ical issue. It was not clear to me what I, as a self-avowed,
practicing, Black-Womanist-Liberationist-Christian
Ethicist, was doing responding to Professor Sanders'
paper. Was I trying to persuade practitioners of Afro-
Christian culture to hold on to this organic concept until
we debunk, unmask, and disentangle the political parameters of gender, class and patriarchal authority in the
Black Church community? Was I trying to convince
white establishment scholars that there is genuine merit
in womanist discourse? Was I trying to rethink my own
previous work about Alice Walker's definition of womanist—a definition that has given new meaning to the
Afro-Christian audience in which I live, move, and have
my being? Was I angry with Cheryl Sanders, the white
academy, or the African-American theological guild?
Well, all of the above.[3]

After sorting through her feelings and explaining why she
finds "womanist" a good name for the ethical and theological
work now being generated by black women, Cannon con-
cludes her response to Sanders with a helpful summary of
where she thinks womanist work now should center:

In essence, a womanist liberation theological ethic places
Black women at the center of human social relations and
ecclesiastical institutions. It critiques the images and paradigms that the Black Church uses to promote or
exclude women. A womanist theo-ethical critique serves
as a model for understanding the silences, limitations
and possibilities of Black women's moral agency, by
identifying Afro-Christian cultural patterns and forms,
perspectives, doctrines, and values that are unique and
peculiar to the Black Church community, in order to
assess the dialectical tensions in Black women's past
social relations as well as our current participation in the
Black Church. A Black womanist liberation Christian
ethic is a critique of all human domination in light of
Black women's experience, a faith praxis that unmasks

whatever threatens the well-being of the poorest woman
of color.[4]

I find this an attractive description, though I note that
Sanders's point about Christology remains untouched.

Womanist scholarship is part, perhaps the leading wave,
of a broad effort to widen the horizons within which feminism,
conceived as the effort to promote the full humanity of
women and their full equality with men, conducts its labors.
As black women seeking liberation interacted with white
women, they often found that solidarity as women was not
enough to overcome differences caused historically by race.
Bluntly put, they found that being feminists did not necessarily free white women of racism. As well, they found that
their own cultural and ecclesiastical situations could differ significantly from those of white women, making it necessary to
qualify many of the propositions that were becoming doctri-
naire in white feminist circles, lest those propositions become
inapplicable to black experience. *Womanist* is a term coined to
protect the integrity, the singularities, of black women's experience. As such, it has been a salutary reminder that women
vary considerably, and that any adequate feminist theology
or ethics has to provide for such variety.

In the same vein, feminists have come to recognize the
unique problems and cultural resources of Hispanic and
Asian women.[5] Also, feminist critiques now tend to be more
sensitive to differences in class than they were a decade ago.
Where one stands on the socio-economic scale has a lot to do
with how one perceives women's needs, pains, possibilities.
The criticism of the women's movement as serving only white,
middle- to upper-class American women has taken hold. Pluralism has become the watchword. Any feminists genuinely
desiring the well-being of all their sisters have to be grateful
for this fact. The more fully we appreciate the distinctive cultural, racial, economic, social, and other factors impinging on
given women's lives, the more likely we shall be to discern
what ideas and practical programs will prove liberating.

Nor may we overlook religious diversity. Within Christianity, black, Hispanic, and Asian traditions obviously can

diverge considerably from one another as well as from white traditions. Looking outside of Christianity, it becomes clear that both feminism and interreligious dialogue will only profit from discussions among feminists of different world-religious traditions. When Hindu and Muslim women speak to one another frankly and lovingly, both their sisterhood and their religious peace will profit. When Christian and Jewish women can discuss both their religious and their sexual situations, including their occasional frictions with one another, feminism and interreligious understanding will advance hand in hand. The same for all the other combinations: Buddhist-Christian dialogue, Muslim-Jewish dialogue, Hindu-Christian dialogue, and more.[6]

Whatever impinges on people's actual identities is relevant to their common task of understanding both themselves and others. Women who can see the impact of their economic situation or their social class on their perceptions of themselves, other women, men, and indeed God, are more likely to liberate themselves from dysfunctional ideas and patterns of behavior than women who cannot. There are no irrelevant factors. For the hard season we are now in, where the task seems to be discovering the full implications of feminism, all participants will be required to bear patiently with ongoing revelations of how much in their lives still awaits redemption, including their interactions as feminists of different backgrounds.

In putting things this way, I want to express great sympathy with those discovering their unique feminist agendas as black, white, poor, rich, Hispanic, Asian, well-educated, poorly educated, straight, lesbian, physically healthy, physically ill, and other "sorts" of women. At the same time I want to suggest that pluralism is not the whole story—not all that appears when we look, not from the middle, but from the end, where we may assume a God's-eye view. Simply as human beings, women and men hold a great many things in common. Simply as women, human beings with female chromosomes, we victims of patriarchy also share a great deal. So, even as we try to honor the diversity of the experiences with which feminism ought to concern itself, making particularities badges of beauty and honor rather than signs of deviance, we do well to retain a sense of the whole—the whole human family, the full company of women, the entire Body of Christ—and a sense of humor, asking how we have managed to screw things up so badly!

I want *feminism* to connote what at its best *catholic* has connoted: thought, practice, sensibility, life directed toward the whole, possessed by a desire to be open to all the manifestations of God's goodness, beauty, and love. I don't want feminism to sanction anything cabined, cribbed, separatist. My ideal feminism does not hate men or blame men for all the ills in creation. Neither does it shrink from demanding that men change their sinful ways, because those ways are hurting their wives, sisters, lovers, daughters, mothers, friends, collaborators—people who should be dear to them, flesh of their flesh and bone of their bone. My ideal feminism takes the experience of women, any woman, much as Katie Cannon takes the experience of black women, as a lens through which to illumine the sufferings of all oppressed peoples.

I believe that our deepest sufferings are the assaults on our hope. When we despair about the human project, or about our own personal projects of becoming mature, fulfilled, wise, helpful, holy, we are in direst straits. To be human is to have hopes, dreams, desires for a better life, a better self, a better community. To be human is to want to make beautiful things and cut down things that are ugly, evil, frustrating, sickening. When women experience that bonding together, making circles of friendship, collaboration, and worship, that restores their hope, recharges their desire to work for a better situation for all people, their experience is redemptive, saving. When they experience that a mystery draws near in their circle, allowing their hopes to broaden to include overcoming death and evil, finitude and ignorance, their experience is mystagogic.

Inasmuch as I have found Christian experience the most mystagogic, I tend to think that Christian experience is the most crucial for women's liberation. I would never say, however, that explicitly, specifically Christian experience is the only liberating mystagogy. There are many ways of meeting the divine mystery, many modes of being taken up into the divine transcendence and so liberated from the limitations of a humanity confined to itself. One of the best marks of true, valid, healthy mystagogy, in fact, is the largeness of heart it inspires. Drawn into the divine largess, the mystic cannot be tiny-hearted, pusillanimous. Such a person must become magnanimous, expanding in love toward the height and depth and length and breadth of the divinity revealing itself. "The world is charged with the grandeur of God." God is always more. Religious feminists have the opportunity to make this majority of God the wellspring of their passion for the liberation of women and the destruction of sinful patriarchies. Feminism at its deepest levels of sympathy and fellow-feeling is manifestly a work of grace.

The Good Conscience

Having treated, however obliquely, the words *Christian* and *feminist* in our preoccupying phrase, we now turn to the word *ethics*. Sidney Callahan offers the following assessment of where the crux of the ethical enterprise—forming people of good conscience—now stands:

> Moral education and an effort to encourage progress toward the freedom, coherence, and committed integrity of the good person is a many-faceted enterprise. Today, the different approaches to moral development need to be unified in a more-adequate holistic model. A conscience curriculum needs to simultaneously engender moral emotions, teach moral reasoning, and convey moral knowledge. Moral education can fail by slighting either the need for critical thinking or the need for personal motivations emerging from empathy, caring, and emotional attachments to a vision of the good. It is difficult to give full weight to everything needed for the successful growth and development of conscience. Many factors operate in the moral enterprise: moral freedom, and human limits, active directed thinking and sponta-

neous preconscious operations, reason and emotion, the individual self and the constitutive community.

In the final analysis, each person runs the course and authors a morality play. Moral communities partially shape self-conscious selves, who become free moral agents selecting and creating a moral world. With large and small moral decisions of conscience, we strengthen, or alternately erode and destroy, moral consciousness — in ourselves, in our families, and in our fellow sojourners. We can usually recognize extremes of moral evil, moral weakness, or moral heroism. In the middle range, we can usually distinguish better moral decisions from those that are worse. Unfortunately, we cannot have infallible, guaranteed moral assessments of the human mind and heart — including our own. The morally wise grow humble and careful, albeit steadfast and firm. The moral quest continues to attract and compel humankind. Conscience holds its own.[7]

Let us begin from the end: "Conscience holds its own." The play on words must be deliberate. Callahan believes that becoming good, living a moral life, has its own intrinsic appeal. We are made to be good, moral, ethical. This idea, quite Confucian, seems to be a matter of observation. As Eric Voegelin has put it mordantly, human beings will not live by depravity alone. Enough in us wants to live in the light to keep the powers of darkness from "comprehending" us totally. (They cannot reach around and embrace us, any more than they can understand our apparently foolish desire to be more than selfish.) So, conscience continues, generation after generation, to press people to be good: honest and loving human beings who honor what is so and offer their fellow creatures shared feeling, compassion, humanity.

Second, conscience holds its own in the sense that those given to it, those determined or graced to be good, gladly stay within its grasp. The Socratic notion that self-knowledge is the key to wisdom and fulfillment plays in this conception. Those who follow conscience slowly learn what they are and what they are not. Kant spoke of the starry heavens above and the moral law within. The second was as mysterious, as wonderful, as the first. Conscience is the awareness that we *ought* to follow the light; honor the truth; render one another justice; hurt not the earth (Rev. 7:3); love God with whole mind, heart, soul, and strength, love our neighbors as ourselves. Where does this awareness come from? Can it suffice for our journey? What do we need to educate ourselves, educate our children, in its imperatives and gifts? Has anything changed from the time of Plato, when Socrates could make do with a negative daimon, feeling free to prosecute any course from which his conscience did not warn him off? What about a Christian conscience? Can we hope that the Spirit of Christ will take over our moral selves, as well as our deepest prayer, making the crucial case for us before God with sighs too deep for words? What is the crucial case we need to make before God? Is it enough that we are trying to be good: attentive, intelligent, reasonable, responsible, loving (Lonergan's transcendental precepts)?

Committing ourselves to living conscientiously does not exempt us from exacting questions. Day by day we have to learn further lessons in what the good conscience, the mind of Christ, actually means. But, for our consolation, we can remind ourselves that we are not alone. Relying on conscience has been a hallowed path. East and West, from Confucianism to Christianity, those walking this path have made morality a matter of honoring the divinity present in the human heart, more intimate to us than we are to ourselves.

In the center of her concluding summary, Callahan bows to the recent interest of ethicists in narrative and says that we each author a morality play. Our biographies are stories. We are the writers and the lead actors. And our stories, our dramatic enactments of our human potential, are fraught with issues of right and wrong. Frighteningly, we can abuse our consciences, our moral selves, and become people who call wrong right, falsehood truth. We can become ideologues, bigots, denizens of what Voegelin called a "secondary reality," concocted with a culpable disregard for such primary realities as our debts to nature and our orientation to God. We can become new gnostics, convinced that Hitler, or Marx, or Stalin, or the latest maven of supply side economics is the eschatological prophet.

Consolingly, however, reality, the handiwork of the living God, offers us correctives. Marxism breaks down, not only because it overvalues ideology but more basically because it tries to veto the idea of God. That cannot be. Nothing is more fundamental or obvious to the healthy human spirit than the fact that we do not explain ourselves. If we are the acme of creation, creation is a complete folly, a full absurdity. Why should creation have begun? To what end do human beings suffer and work? Jean-Paul Sartre thought we are but useless passions. If there is no God, if the universe remains unexplained by a mystery more holy (more real) than itself, Jean-Paul Sartre is correct.

A conscience careful about its experiences, concerned to discern the movements of the heart, finds that Sartre must be wrong. The world is admirable, despite so much in its human sectors that we must despise. The positive exceeds the negative, because being is more fundamental than non-being, including most pertinently the non-being of moral evil.

So the morality play of which we are the authors deals with age-old themes. We shall do well to match the depth of Aeschylus and Mencius, let alone the depth of Second-Isaiah and Mark. Like it or not, we shall one day walk a way we would not have chosen, as Peter and Jesus did. We shall die, and we can only hope it will not be in agony. What we have become by the moment of our death will be the denouement of our morality play in the eyes of the world, probably even in our own eyes. But perhaps not in the eyes of God. Perhaps, in the eyes of God, even when our hearts condemn us, there is something greater. The benefit of focusing the imperatives of the ethical life on human conscience is forcing people to take responsibility for their moral selves—making them take their freedom in hand, own up to the choices time lays out before them. The liability can be remaining within a humanistic framework that takes no account of God and grace.

On our own we are depressing. There is no health in us, as more people than the Calvinists have seen. Unless God is greater than our hearts, more ultimate than our consciences, there is no gospel, no divine comedy, no resurrection as a stunning reversal of everything prudent, calculable, likely on human terms. God can make all things new. If we are to accredit Christian Scripture, God has made all things new, and death is now no more. But this is the babble of faith, the murmur of mystics, the patois of people who love what eye has not seen, ear not heard, what has not entered the human heart to conceive. This is the conviction of saints like Augustine, who solve the whole problem of conscience, of becoming a good human being, with a single pithy imperative: Love and do what you will. Ah, sweet mystery.

Models

In thinking about Christian feminist ethicists whom I might propose as models of what the three words, properly joined, should be, I turn to three Warren Lecturers at the University of Tulsa, women who have been committed Christian feminists working on ethical matters. Perhaps it is fitting to conclude this extended essay with a reflection on what their lectures, and they themselves, have taught me.

Anne Patrick's lecture, "Conscience and Community: Catholic Moral Theology Today," offers an obvious bridge to Callahan's concern for the formation of good consciences. Among Patrick's many noteworthy sentences stand the following:

> Conscience is a highly valued term in our culture, and it is something we treasure. Few would disagree with St. Thomas Aquinas' judgment that "anyone upon whom the ecclesiastical authority, in ignorance of true facts, imposes a demand that offends against his [sic] clear conscience, should perish in excommunication rather than violate his conscience." We resonate more and more with John Henry Newman's observation in his famous letter to the Duke of Norfolk, where he stated with respect to papal infallibility that "Certainly, if I am obliged to bring religion into after-dinner toasts, (which

indeed does not seem quite the thing) I shall drink, —
to the Pope, if you please, — still, Conscience first, and
to the Pope afterwards." . . .

But surely we know of many instances where conscience is clear, but behavior questionable or evil. Theologian Daniel Maguire is wise to insist that "To the
general statement that one should always follow one's
conscience should be added that one should always
question one's conscience. The autonomy of conscience
is not absolute." . . .

And this is where the Church can function so positively in our moral lives. The Church does not supply
the perfect answer to all our moral questions, but it gives
us a community where faithful moral reasoning can go
on, always with attention to the values Jesus cherished,
and with confidence in his continued presence in our
midst. In addition, the Church gives us saints to inspire
us, friends to support us, spiritual guides to assist us,
and teachers to challenge and instruct us. Properly
understood and exercised, the Church's teaching
authority is a marvelous gift for our moral and spiritual
development, for it offers the wisdom gained from centuries of experience with the human heart to individuals
who might otherwise have to reinvent the ethical wheel
for themselves.[8]

The Church is indeed limited and fallible, but also extremely helpful. The community of Christ is flawed, especially
in matters of sexual morality and the treatment of women,
but it possesses treasures of grace and tradition sufficient to
offset its own flaws. To overlook these treasures, this wealth
of experience, is to cut oneself off from gifts of God.

Too many of the feminist ethicists I have surveyed seem to
be reinventing the wheel. In their rush to correct biases deriving from patriarchy, they exalt their own experience far
higher than it deserves. Clearly patriarchy needs all the cor-
rection, the overcoming, that feminists can muster. Equally
clearly, however, the Church is much more than a patriarchy
(if only because women have always been a majority of its

membership), and feminism is a highly suspect religion. To expect women's experience to hoist the full load of divine revelation is to show oneself either terribly naive or terribly proud.

Mary Ann Hinsdale is like Anne Patrick in striving for a balanced Christian feminist ethics. She wants both the sharp edge of prophecy and the calm center of faith in a God, a Christ, who finally blunts all our anxieties. She wants the Christian community to welcome the full contribution of women, but she thinks of that contribution as an offering not only to women but also to men. The three components of the moral vision that I have been pursuing—its Christianity, feminism, and ethics—cohere admirably in the following paragraphs:

> The dream of Christian feminists is for a Church which is equal, which includes the gifts of women's leadership, recognizes their voices, heals their pain, and celebrates their desires. It is a dream which one can find in the Scriptures but not in the present concrete structuring of the Church. Though the New Testament depicts women as disciples, tells of households of inclusivity, speaks of women as ecclesial leaders and women serving as prophets, the current reality is that women find only partial acceptance as full members of the community of Jesus' disciples. . . .
> Women-Church is not "for women only," but for women and men who wish to speak together words of emancipatory transformation. Women-Church is the questioning of new possibilities, the experimentation with new forms, the envisioning of new relations. Using the filters of difference, specificity, embodiment, solidarity, anticipation, and transformation, it asks, "What is the Church? What happens when the Church experiments with models of community rather than securing structures of bureaucracy? What occurs when the Church is the embodiment of emancipatory transformation in its life together and in its mission, rather than

the instantiation of private religious experience and occasional acts of charity?"[9]

I think that what occurs is a lilt of desire breathed into us by the Holy Spirit. We sense, glimpse, hear as prevenient thunder the possibilities God has unleashed by raising Jesus the Christ. We shake off the chains that have been binding our imaginations. We let our minds and hearts expand to match the wideness of God's mercy. And we realize, if we are theologically astute, that when people understand the essentials of their faith, they are poised to exercise the liberty of the children of God.

When people know how and why the Trinity, Grace, and the Incarnation function as the three cardinal Christian mysteries, the inmost structure of the reality faith finds in the resurrected Christ, then how they assemble, how they distribute and share power, what songs they sing and creeds they recite become not irrelevant, but supple, free, directed lightly by an indwelling Spirit who teaches them the proper sense in which all expressions of faith are symbolic.

Such expressions can change, as the needs of an evolutionary history require. They can bend and shift to accommodate new social awarenesses, like those now carried by feminism, new cultural opportunities, like those now presented by the Church's reception in Asia and Africa. The rigidity, hierarchical patterns of thought, and suspiciously advantageous (self-serving) hideboundedness of current patriarchal conceptions of the Church stand revealed as unnecessary, even unfaithful. Finally, and amusingly, such a grasp of the essentials of Christian faith, such a being grasped by the Spirit of Christ, also makes shrewd believers free of what might be called the ideology of progressives. If the Spirit takes us out of fossilized forms that owe too much to the past, the Spirit also takes us out of any slavery to current fashions, new notions, political correctness. Behold, God makes all things new. This newness placed by God at the center of the Church is distinctive for its humility and love, for its lack of ego and wealth of good will.

My last model is Rosemary Haughton, who, in her usual

quiet way, gave one of the most prophetic lectures I have ever heard. Once again, a few paragraphs suggest the flavor and savor of a mature Christian feminist ethics:

So the role of the prophet is two-fold—to call to anger and grief and repentance, and exemplify these experiences, and to energize by the call to see visions and make them a reality.

Neither of these activities makes prophets popular with the political or religious establishment, and we see in the life and death of Jesus the enactment of the prophet's role, leading to such a surge of fear and hate that nothing but his death would serve to remove the threat. Jesus denounced the evils he saw, driven by compassion founded on a very clear and accurate social analysis, but he also announced the vision of the reign of God and called people to begin, at once, to live by that reality which he saw as already operative, though its fullness was yet to come. He surrounded himself with a motley collection of men and women who lived out a very different set of relationships from the accepted ones—eating together without class distinction, working together as friends, including women in discipleship and mission, learning to approach God intimately as children by passing and even setting aside aspects of the codes and customs which had been built up to preserve the economic and social status quo.

But Jesus was more than a prophet. Studying and reflecting on the message of his prophetic forbears, his own vision transcended theirs, because it responded to a different reality. The prophets of old called Israel back to her ancient vows and saw the renewed nation as a focus of regeneration for the world. Jesus saw that vision too, but he operated from a much wider and more informed perception of the world. It grew to envisage something more than the concept of Jerusalem as the center of newness—indeed he came to realize that doom lay on this beloved city, the rot had gone too far. Instead, he saw that center, as it were, dispersed, a gathering of the peoples of the earth into a newness that could be universal. And for that vision, a different prophetic role was needed—not just individual prophets, but something more. He himself accepted and lived a prophetic role but he did not appoint followers as prophets, as Elijah called Elisha or Jeremiah inspired Baruch. Rather, he created a new kind of prophetic entity, a community of people whose very existence constituted prophecy. They would not only preach the universal mercy of God and the call to newness of life, they would demonstrate it. The way they lived would be their most important prophetic task.

"Call no man father"—the new community would certainly include men who were fathers, as it included women who were mothers, and there must be real and effective leadership—but no patriarchs, no dominance and subordination; leadership must be that of empowerment and service, not "lording it over" other people "as the heathens do." They were to live as friends, transcending but of course including family ties.[10]

Based in the reality of Jesus, filled with the Spirit of Jesus, Christian feminist ethics could find few slogans better than "to live as friends." The equality and love that inspired Jesus, that came to voice in his preaching, can create the community for which our hearts long. Whatever brings us nearer to that community is Christian, feminist, and ethical in one. Whatever takes us away from it is the enemy of Christian faith, feminist commitment, ethical maturity and wisdom. That community has a place for anger, as the ministry of Jesus did, but anger does not rule its awareness. It has a larger place for peace and joy, because these are the gifts of the risen Christ, the signs of the paschal Spirit. But its largest place, its seat of honor among the virtues, is reserved for love, as all Christian ethicists concede. Bound to the New Testament—committed to the twofold commandment of Jesus as the summary of the Law and the Prophets, to the Pauline teaching in 1 Corinthians 13 about the more excellent way, and to the Johannine equation of God and love—all Christian ethicists have to make love the preeminent virtue.

Can feminist ethicists do the same? The verdict is not yet in, but I find many reasons for thinking they can. Women know a great deal about love, not because the cultural stereotype is that we are more romantic than men, but because women know a great deal about the hungers, pains, and hopes of the human heart, which boil down to love. Christians believe that all people are made for a God of love, that all mature souls are naturally Christian. We need only apply this humanistic tradition to today's feminists to find a priori, theological reasons for listening carefully to what feminists have to say, straining hard to hear women's cries of pain and insight. The more we translate these cries into the language of love—love sought and love found—the more we shall overcome the current division, both large and lamentable, between secular feminism and traditional Christianity.

Mutually, dialectically, feminists and Christians might challenge one another to become better lovers of the full reality laid out for humankind: nature, society, ourselves, divinity. I can foresee nothing more exciting, profitable, or enjoyable than an ethical future in which such a challenge became the congenial, serious play of both the camps to which I pledge allegiance. Amen.

Notes

Chapter 1: Introduction

1. Ellen Gilchrist, *The Anna Papers* (Boston: Little Brown, 1988), p. 16.
2. Marilyn Pearsall, *Women and Values: Readings in Recent Feminist Philosophy* (Belmont, CA: Wadsworth, 1986), p. 266.
3. Margaret A. Farley, "Feminist Ethics," in *The Westminster Dictionary of Christian Ethics*, ed. James F. Childress and John Macquarrie (Philadelphia: Westminster, 1986), p. 229.
4. Ibid., p. 231.
5. Vincent McNamara, "Moral Life, Christian," in *The New Dictionary of Theology*, ed. Joseph A. Komonchak, Mary Collins, and Dermot Lane (Wilmington, DE: Michael Glazier, 1987), p. 677.
6. Joann Wolski Conn, *Women's Spirituality: Resources for Christian Development* (New York: Paulist Press, 1986), p. 3.
7. Nancy C. Ring, "Doctrine," in *The New Dictionary of Theology*, p. 293.

Chapter 2: Commitment and Discernment

1. Margaret Farley, *Personal Commitments* (San Francisco: Harper & Row, 1990), pp. 15-16.
2. Ibid., p. 10.
3. On the question of Jesus, see Anne E. Carr, *Transforming Grace* (San Francisco: Harper & Row, 1988), pp. 158-200.
4. Mary E. Hunt, *Fierce Tenderness* (New York: Crossroad, 1991), p. 150.
5. Ibid., p. 89.
6. Elisabeth Schüssler Fiorenza, *Bread Not Stone* (Boston: Beacon Press, 1984), pp. 86-87.
7. Rosemary Haughton, *Song in a Strange Land* (Springfield, IL: Templegate, 1990), pp. 171-172.

8. Ibid., pp. 170-171.

9. Jane Smiley, *Ordinary Love and Good Will* (New York: Alfred A. Knopf, 1990), p. 74.

10. Ibid., pp. 77, 75.

Chapter 3: Social Ethics

1. Maria Riley, O.P., "Feminist Analysis: A Missing Perspective," in *The Logic of Solidarity*, ed. Gregory Baum and Robert Ellsberg (Maryknoll, NY: Orbis Books, 1989), p. 200.

2. Ibid., p. 199.

3. Joan Walsh, "Setting the Scene," in *A Cry for Justice*, ed. Robert McAfee Brown and Sydney Thompson Brown (New York: Paulist Press, 1989), pp. 20-21.

4. Ibid., p. 21.

5. Karen Lebacqz, *Justice in an Unjust World* (Minneapolis: Augsburg, 1987), pp. 60-61.

6. Judith Plaskow, "Anti-Semitism: The Unacknowledged Racism," in *Women's Consciousness, Women's Conscience*, ed. Barbara Hilkert Andersen, et al. (San Francisco: Harper & Row, 1987), p. 79.

7. See Judith Plaskow, *Standing Again at Sinai* (San Francisco: Harper & Row, 1990).

8. Toinette M. Eugene, "While Love Is Unfashionable: An Exploration of Black Spirituality and Sexuality," in *Women's Consciousness, Women's Conscience*, p. 136.

9. Consuela del Prado, "I Sense God in Another Way," in *Through Her Eyes: Women's Theology from Latin America*, ed. Elsa Tamez (Maryknoll, NY: Orbis Books, 1989), pp. 141-42.

10. Ivone Gebara and Maria Clara Bingemer, *Mary: Mother of God, Mother of the Poor* (Maryknoll, NY: Orbis Books, 1989), p. 161.

11. United Nations, *The World's Women 1970-1990: Trends and Statistics* (New York: United Nations, 1991), p. 73.

Chapter 4: Sexual Morality

1. Aruna Gnanadason, "Women's Oppression: A Sinful Situation," in *With Passion and Compassion*, ed. Virginia Fabella and Mercy Amba Oduyoye (Maryknoll, NY: Orbis Books, 1988), pp. 69-70.

2. See Elaine Pagels, *Adam, Eve, and the Serpent* (New York: Random House, 1988); also Elizabeth A. Clark, *Women in the Early Church* (Wilmington, DE: Michael Glazier, 1983).

3. Alicia Partnoy, *The Little School* (Pittsburgh: Cleis Press, 1985),

p. 15, quoted in Paula M. Cooey, "The Redemption of the Body," in *After Patriarchy*, ed. Paula M. Cooey, William R. Eakin, and Jay B. McDaniel (Maryknoll, NY: Orbis Books, 1991), pp. 109-110.

4. Cooey, pp. 111-112.

5. Ibid., p. 121.

6. For one exterior debate, with Cardinal Josef Tomko, see Denise Lardner Carmody, "No, Yes, and No," in *Christian Mission and Interreligious Dialogue*, ed. Paul Mojzes and Leonard Swidler (Lewiston, ME: Edwin Mellen, 1990), pp. 42-50.

7. Rita Nakashima Brock, "And A Little Child Will Lead Us: Christology and Child Abuse," in *Christianity, Patriarchy, and Abuse*, ed. Joanne Carlson Brown and Carole R. Bohn (New York: Pilgrim Press, 1989), pp. 51-52. See also Rosemary Radford Ruether, "The Western Religious Tradition and Violence Against Women in the Home," ibid., pp. 31-41.

8. Carter Heyward, *Speaking of Christ*, ed. Ellen C. Davis (New York: Pilgrim Press, 1989), pp. 24-25.

9. Lisa Sowle Cahill, "Marriage: Institution, Relationship, Sacrament," in *One Hundred Years of Catholic Social Thought*, ed. John A. Coleman (Maryknoll, NY: Orbis Books, 1991), p. 117.

10. Ibid., pp. 117-118.

11. Beverly Wildung Harrison, "Theology and Morality of Procreative Choice," in *Making the Connections*, ed. Carol S. Robb (Boston: Beacon Press, 1985), pp. 132-133. See also Beverly Wildung Harrison, *Our Right to Choose* (Boston: Beacon Press, 1983).

12. Denise Lardner Carmody, *The Double Cross: Ordination, Abortion, and Catholic Feminism* (New York: Crossroad, 1986).

Chapter 5: Ecclesiastical Issues

1. Phyllis Trible, *Texts of Terror* (Philadelphia: Fortress, 1984), pp. 1-2.

2. Ibid., pp. 4-5.

3. Mary Gordon, "The Gospel According to Saint Mark," in *Incarnation*, ed. Alfred Corn (New York: Viking, 1990), pp. 16-17.

4. Marjorie Proctor-Smith, "Images of Women in the Lectionary," in *Women: Invisible in Church and Theology*, ed. Elisabeth Schüssler Fiorenza and Mary Collins (Nijmegen and Edinburgh: Sichting Concilium and T & T Clark, 1985), pp. 58-59.

5. Mary Collins, "The Refusal of Women in Clerical Circles," in *Women in the Church, I*, ed. Madonna Kolbenschlag (Washington, D.C.: The Pastoral Press, 1987), p. 52.

6. Ibid., p. 59.

7. Rosemary Radford Ruether, *Women-Church: Theology and Practice* (San Francisco: Harper & Row, 1988), pp. 57-59.

8. Joan Chittister, "The Fullness of Grace," in *Cloud of Witnesses*, ed. Jim Wallis and Joyce Hollyday (Maryknoll, NY and Washington, D.C.: Orbis Books and Sojourners, 1991), p. 186.

9. See Denise Lardner Carmody, *The Double Cross* (New York: Crossroad, 1986), pp. 17-75.

10. James J. Kenneally, *The History of American Catholic Women* (New York: Crossroad, 1990), pp. 118-119.

11. Monika K. Hellwig, *Christian Women in a Troubled World* (New York: Paulist Press, 1985), pp. 24-27.

12. Sandra M. Schneiders, *Beyond Patching: Faith and Feminism in the Catholic Church* (New York: Paulist Press, 1991), pp. 110-112.

13. Sallie McFague, *Models of God* (Philadelphia: Fortress, 1987), pp. 149-150.

Chapter 6: Conclusion

1. Rita Nakashima Brock, *Journeys by Heart: A Christology of Erotic Power* (New York: Crossroad, 1988), p. 52.

2. Cheryl J. Sanders, "Roundtable Discussion: Christian Ethics and Theology in Womanist Perspective," *Journal of Feminist Studies in Religion*, vol. 5, no. 2 (Fall 1989), 90-91.

3. Katie G. Cannon, "Response," ibid., p. 92.

4. Ibid., p. 92. See also Delores S. Williams, "Womanist Theology," in *Weaving the Visions*, ed. Judith Plaskow and Carol P. Christ (San Francisco: Harper & Row, 1989), pp. 179-186.

5. See Ada Maria Isasi-Diaz, "Toward an Understanding of Feminismo Hispaño in the U.S.A.," in *Women's Consciousness and Women's Conscience*, ed. Barbara Hilkert Androlsen, Christine E. Gudorf, and Mary D. Pellauer (San Francisco: Harper & Row, 1985), pp. 51-61; also Virginia Fabella and Mercy Amba Oduyoye, *With Passion and Compassion: Third World Women Doing Theology* (Maryknoll, NY: Orbis Books, 1988).

6. See Maura O'Neill, *Women Speaking, Women Listening: Women in Interreligious Dialogue* (Maryknoll, NY: Orbis Books, 1988).

7. Sidney Callahan, *In Good Conscience* (San Francisco: Harper San Francisco, 1991), pp. 213-214. See also Sharon Welch, "Ideology and Social Change," in *Weaving the Visions*, pp. 336-343, and Martha T. Mednick, "On the Politics of Psychological Constructs," *American Psychologist*, vol. 44, no. 8 (August 1989), 1118-1123.

8. Anne E. Patrick, "Conscience and Community: Catholic Moral Theology Today" (University of Tulsa: Warren Center for Catholic Studies, 1989), pp. 8-10.

9. Mary Ann Hinsdale, "Power and Participation in the Church: Voices from the Margins" (University of Tulsa: Warren Center for Catholic Studies, 1990), pp. 8-9.

10. Rosemary Haughton, "The Church as Prophet: Challenge and Judgement" (University of Tulsa: Warren Center for Catholic Studies, 1989), p. 3.

Acknowledgments

Index